A faith like mine

LONDON, NEW YORK,
MELBOURNE, MUNICH, AND DELHI

Editor Susannah Steel
Designer Claire Legemah
Senior editor Fran Jones
Art editors Sheila Collins, Jacqui Swan
Managing editor Linda Esposito
Managing art editor Jane Thomas
US editor Margaret Parrish
Publishing managers Caroline Buckingham,
Andrew Macintyre
Art director Simon Webb
DTP designer Siu Yin Chan
Picture research Fran Vargo
DK picture library Karl Stange
Production controller Ally Lenane

Consultant Dr. Peter Connolly

First American Edition, 2005
Published in the United States by
DK Publishing Inc.
375 Hudson Street,
New York, New York 10014

06 07 08 09 10 9 8 7 6 5 4 3 2

A Cataloging-in-Publication record for this book is available from the Library of Congress.

ISBN 0-7566-1975-0

Color reproduction by Colourscan, Singapore

Printed and bound in China by Leo Paper Products Limited

Discover more at **www.dk.com**

A faith like mine

A celebration of the world's religions—seen through the eyes of children

Laura Buller

Contents

Shivani from Australia, page 18

Jang-chub from Tibet, page 24

Hasini from Sri Lanka, page 30

Gurkaran from India, page 40

Dan from Argentina,
page 45

Antonino from Italy,
page 54

Corinne from Sweden,
page 56

Rachid from Morocco,
page 64

Yasmin from the UK,
page 67

What is faith?

WHEN YOU TRUST SOMETHING, you have faith in it. If you believe something to be true, you show your faith by being loyal to it. For millions of people across the globe, their faith is the thing they trust, hold true, and are loyal to. They pray and worship, and read the words that help them to remain faithful. The children in this book will tell you why their faith is important to them.

A Sikh family shows their faith by leaving their hair uncut.

Faith and family

Your parents probably passed their faith on to you. You may have been part of your religion since you were a small baby. As you grow older, you may experience some of the same religious rites and ceremonies that were special to your parents. You will be able to understand the role that faith plays in your family.

Words of faith

Before writing was invented, people passed on their faith through their words and actions. The teachings and ideas behind some of the world's faiths were eventually written down. Most faiths have a book or books that tell the story of that faith and that guide people to follow the right path in life. You may have heard stories from one of these books.

Hindu scriptures are shown here, written down in the ancient Sanskrit language.

Faith and tradition

A tradition is a custom that has been handed down through generations. Traditions are really important, especially for children, because it is good to know what to expect. Faith may be a big part of your family tradition. For example, your family might gather to do special things, or share certain foods, when you celebrate a religious tradition together.

These boys in Guatemala wear traditional robes and carry an incense burner in a Christian Holy Week parade.

Faith and learning

Getting an education is an important goal for most children. It helps make them better able to understand the world around them. Some people think it is just as important to see the world through the beliefs and practices of their faith, so many children around the world attend religious schools. They learn to explore their faiths and understand its traditions as they study other subjects.

A new Jewish synagogue in Istanbul, Turkey

Faith and community

Along with your immediate family, faith can bring together a larger "family" of people with common beliefs. This is the religious community. While faith can be something private and special just to you, many people like to share their faith with others by attending a religious service.

Muslim girls read the Qur'an in Nigeria.

Buddhists at a funeral in Vietnam

Faith and hope

Today, we know the answers to a lot of questions about how the world works. Yet many things in life are still a mystery. Why do bad things happen? What happens to us after we die? Faith offers answers to these questions. Some religions say we have souls that will live again as another living thing. Others say our souls will go to Heaven if we are good. Knowing what to expect when our life on Earth ends gives us hope for the future.

Traditional beliefs

FROM THE TIME when the earliest humans looked up at the stars at night and wondered who made them, people have looked for answers through faith. Historians think that the idea of practicing a religion is very old indeed. Some of these early faiths died out as empires fell and newer religions took hold. Other ancient religious rituals live on. Traditional faiths all share a common belief in powerful spirits that can change or shape lives.

Ancient religions

There are some very old religions that are no longer practiced. Ancient people once worshiped gods and goddesses, held festivals and rituals, and made offerings. We know this because they left artifacts behind, such as this Egyptian painting of Horus, the sky god.

Natural world

Many people believe in the power of the natural world. This Australian aboriginal painting shows what is called the dreamtime—a time long ago when all living things were made. Aboriginals believe they have occupied Australia since the beginning of time. Their connection to the land, its plants, and animals affects every aspect of their culture.

Masked shaman dances in Sri Lanka

World of spirits

Many traditional religions are based on a belief that powerful, invisible beings live all around us. These spirits are everywhere, and they can affect everyone's life. People try to talk to the spirits and make offerings to them. They may do this through a shaman, a priest and healer. People believe that if the spirits are happy, good things will happen.

Rites and rituals

There are special ceremonies in all religions to mark the major milestones in life, from birth to death. There are also religious festivals to mark big events in the history of a religion, or to celebrate a new year or season. Singing, music, and dancing are often included in these ceremonies. These Native American boys are taking part in a ritual dance at a powwow (tribal gathering).

Sacred places

Mount Fuji (above) in Japan is sacred to followers of the Shinto faith. They believe that the mountain is not only home to several gods, but also the center of the universe. Most religions give certain places, such as natural wonders, or important temples and shrines, a special meaning. People believe that powerful spirits live in these places.

Native American boys wear traditional tribal clothes

Ancestor worship

Many followers of traditional faiths believe that it is important to honor their ancestors. This is because their spirits never die, but live on in the spirit world. Carvings, like this Yoruba figure, are one way to respect the spirits of their ancestors. People hope that their ancestor spirits will influence more powerful spirits to look after them.

Clay ancestor statue from the Yoruba people of Nigeria

Religions around the world

WHERE IN THE WORLD do followers of the main religions live? This map provides a visual guide to those faiths. The colors on the map represent the main religion in each country, but that does not tell the whole story. While Christianity is still the world's largest religion, for example, other religions such as Islam, Hinduism, and Buddhism are growing quickly. Not everyone believes in a God, or follows a religion. Many millions of people in the world are nonreligious.

Many faces, many faiths

Around the world, people often live in societies where there is a mix of different nationalities and faiths. Living in a mixed culture can encourage people to learn about and respect other religions. Reading the words of the children in this book will help open up the world's faiths to you. Even though you may not agree with some of the beliefs, you should be tolerant of them. Everyone has the right to express his or her beliefs.

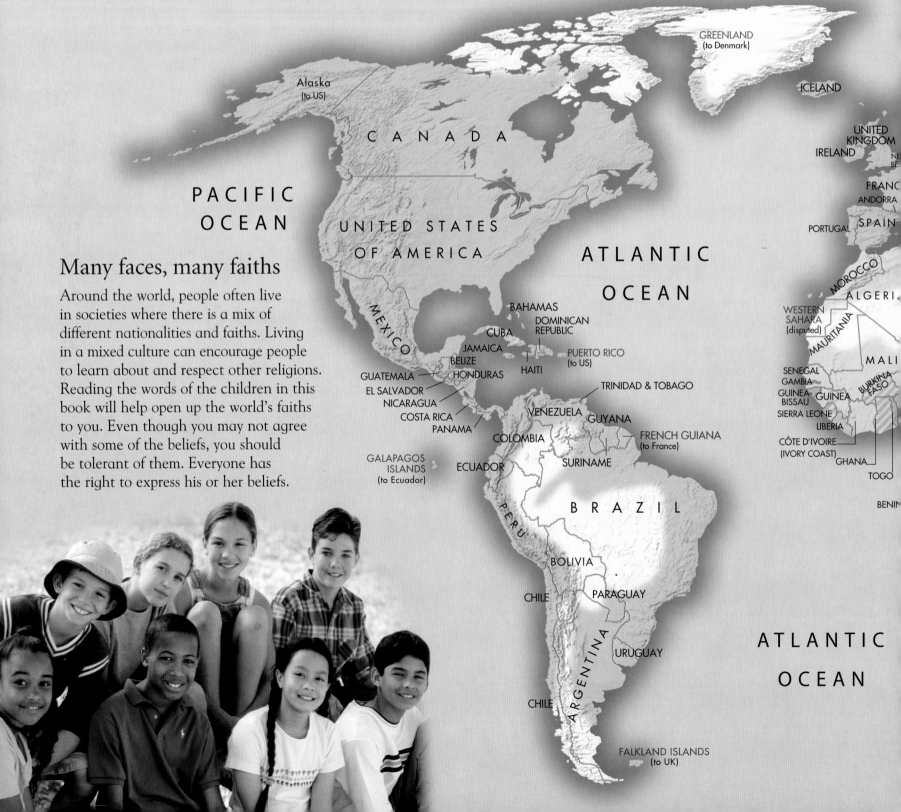

GREENLAND
(to Denmark)

ICELAND

Alaska
(to US)

CANADA

UNITED
KINGDOM
IRELAND
NE
BE

PACIFIC
OCEAN

UNITED STATES
OF AMERICA

ATLANTIC

OCEAN

FRANC
ANDORRA

SPAIN

PORTUGAL

MOROCCO

ALGERI

WESTERN
SAHARA
(disputed)

MAURITANIA

MALI

BAHAMAS

DOMINICAN
REPUBLIC

CUBA

JAMAICA

BELIZE

HONDURAS

HAITI

PUERTO RICO
(to US)

MEXICO

GUATEMALA

EL SALVADOR

NICARAGUA

COSTA RICA

PANAMA

COLOMBIA

TRINIDAD & TOBAGO

VENEZUELA

GUYANA

FRENCH GUIANA
(to France)

SURINAME

SENEGAL
GAMBIA
GUINEA-
BISSAU   GUINEA
SIERRA LEONE

CÔTE D'IVOIRE
(IVORY COAST)

LIBERIA

BURKINA
FASO

GHANA

TOGO

GALAPAGOS
ISLANDS
(to Ecuador)

ECUADOR

PERU

BRAZIL

BENIN

BOLIVIA

CHILE

PARAGUAY

ARGENTINA

URUGUAY

ATLANTIC

OCEAN

CHILE

FALKLAND ISLANDS
(to UK)

Spreading the word

The major faiths have spread across the globe from the places where they were founded in a number of different ways. Immigration (leaving your country to move to another) is one way that religion spreads, as people take their beliefs with them. Missionary groups may travel to other lands seeking to convert people to their faith. In earlier times, military conquests or trade routes helped religions to take hold in different places.

KEY TO THE WORLD'S RELIGIONS

- Christianity
- Islam
- Buddhism
- Hinduism
- Judaism
- Sikhism
- Traditional beliefs
- Nonreligious
- Uninhabited region

Compare these color keys with those on the large world map to see which is the main religion in each country. The map is designed to show the spread of the world's faiths. In some places, such as India, most of the people follow a single religion, Hinduism. In other countries, a striped pattern of two colors shows that there is a mix, such as Christianity and Islam in Nigeria. Some areas, such as China, are mainly nonreligious. The small maps that feature on the introduction to each main faith will tell you the numbers of believers.

Symbol

This symbol is the written form of the most sacred sound in Hinduism, aum, or om. Aum represents the sound of God and means everything—past, present, and future. At the start of every day, and before and after prayers or rituals, Hindus say or sing this sacred sound aloud.

Holy book

The oldest Hindu sacred writings are a set of four books called the Vedas. Veda means "vision" or "wisdom," and Hindus believe that the prayers and hymns contained in the Vedas are revelations from gods.

Krishna is shown with deep blue skin because his name means the color of the night sky

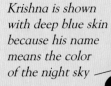

Krishna

Hinduism

MORE THAN 5,000 years ago, the faith known as Hinduism began in India. It evolved out of the many different practices of the Ancient Indian people. So, Hinduism is not a single religion, but a family of religious traditions. Although they show their faith in different ways, most Hindus believe in God, who is worshipped in many forms. They also believe in rebirth in a new body.

Sacred animal

These children in Nepal are reaching out to touch a sacred cow for good luck. Hinduism teaches that every life is sacred. Cows are especially holy, so they are treated with great respect.

God's different names and forms

Most Hindus believe that God is everywhere. Everything in nature is part of God, as are the hundreds of gods and goddesses (who look like people or animals) that Hindus may choose to worship. One way in which God is revealed is as a trio of gods: Brahma, who creates life; Shiva, who makes room for new life; and Vishnu, who keeps things alive. Today, Brahma is not worshipped in the same way as other gods because his work— the world's creation—is done.

Brahma has four faces, one to speak each of the four Vedas.

Shiva the destroyer dances in a circle of fire.

Popular gods and goddesses

Many Hindus worship a god because he or she is special to their family or controls a particular aspect of life.

AGNI	The god of fire and guardian of homes
DEVI	The mother goddess
GANESH	The god of success
KRISHNA	The god of love and divine joy
PARVATI	The goddess of love
SARASVATI	The goddess of truth and wisdom
SHIVA	The god of destruction and re-creation
SRI-LAKSHMI	The goddess of money and beauty
VISHNU	The god of protection and preservation

Ganesh has an elephant's head.

How Hindus worship

Hindu worship is called *puja*. Hindus believe that God is in everything, so they honor and worship God in every aspect of life. They also worship at shrines at home and in buildings called temples. At the heart of every shrine or temple is an image of a god or goddess. Hindus believe that the gods live within the shrines and that viewing their image is the same as being with them. Hindus pray, sing, and make offerings to their favorite god.

This home shrine honors Vishnu, considered a lucky god.

Holy rivers and pilgrimages

Rivers are sacred places to many Hindus. The act of bathing in a river cleans the body as well as the spirit, helping to wash away sins. In India, the most famous holy river is the Ganges. Thousands of Hindus come to this river on a pilgrimage, a special journey to a sacred place.

Pilgrims gather on the banks of the Ganges River in Varanasi, northern India.

Rites of passage

Hindu children are born into their faith. Important ceremonies include a blessing after the birth, a naming ceremony by a priest, and shaving the head for spiritual purification.

Where Hindus live

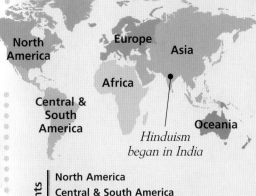

Hinduism began in India

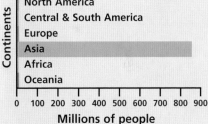

The vast majority of Hindus—about 95 percent of the faith's population—live in India. There are also other substantial Hindu communities in Africa, Europe, and North America.

Main festivals

Holi Spring festival, Hindu New Year *February/March*
Mahasivaratri Festival of Shiva *March*
Ram Navami Celebrates Rama's birthday *April*
Janamashtami Celebrates Krishna's birthday *August*
Navaratri Nine nights' worship of goddess Durga *September/October*
Dussehra Celebrates Rama's life *the day after the end of Navaratri*
Divali Festival of light *October/November*

Aman from India

Divali

A FESTIVAL OF LIGHTS

MY NAME IS AMAN, and I am 13. I enjoy art and playing the keyboard and guitar. I love playing sports, especially cricket. I might be a cricket player when I grow up. To me, the best thing about Hinduism is that we are free to follow our faith as we want. It is a tolerant religion. My favorite festival is Divali. Everyone is happy on this day, and streets and homes are full of lights and sounds.

Divali celebrates the return of King Rama.

We celebrate the night Rama returned home after defeating the evil Ravana. We fill our streets with lights to guide Rama and his wife home.

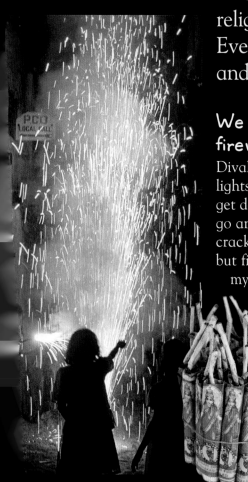

We let off lots of fireworks at night.

Divali is the festival of lights. When it starts to get dark, I can't wait to go and let off fire crackers with my friends, but first I pray with my grandparents.

Bundle of Divali fireworks

Lakshmi, the goddess of wealth

We paint colorful patterns called rangoli.

I help my mother make flower rangolis outside our doors. The patterns welcome guests and also the goddess Lakshmi. A visit from Lakshmi means a good year is ahead.

UK

I love celebrating Diwali in England because when you put the candles around the house it stands out from ALL the other houses in the street and it looks so beautiful.

Shubhi

Canada

My responsibility at Divali, as daughter of the house, is to place diyas around at home and light the first one. I think about Lakshmi and how the light will lead her to our home. Divali is a way for me to understand my Indian religion in a another country.

Aashti

Holi festival

Another popular festival is Holi, which remembers the tricks that the god Krishna played. People play tricks on each other and there are noisy parades. The best part is throwing colored powder at one another and having water fights.

I like giving candy at Divali.

We don't have to go to school at Divali. Instead, we visit each other's homes and take boxes of candy to eat. Everybody greets each other very happily. My family, like many others, wears new clothes on this day.

These dark candies are called gulab jamuns

Our house looks beautiful lit up with diyas

We send cards to our families.

Divali lasts for five days, but not all our family and friends live near enough to visit. We send them Divali cards to wish them a happy year ahead.

Our houses are filled with light.

We use oil lamps and small pots filled with oil, called diyas. This year, I painted several diyas in bright colors and decorated them. We put rows of diyas on the window ledges and balconies of our house. Then we went outside to look at our house. I thought it looked beautiful.

A Hindu girl holds an earthenware diya.

Places to pray

WORSHIP AT SHRINES AND TEMPLES

Tara from the US

MY NAME IS TARA. I am eight years old, and I like horse riding. I am also learning to play the piano. I'm fascinated by all the different Hindu gods. My mother reads me many stories about them. We have a shrine at home, and we go to the temple for special occasions, like Divali. Hindus can pray anywhere, not just at shrines. I say my prayers in bed before I sleep.

Our home shrine is in my mom's room. It is where we pray on special days. My mom keeps a few statues of gods and a diya. When we pray, the diya is lit to symbolize enlightenment.

After worship, we are given a tilak. This red mark on the forehead is made with red powder or sandalwood paste. It helps us to focus on our goals for the day.

A mother and daughter worship at a home shrine.

Before we go to the temple, we buy offerings for the gods.

Inside the temple, we offer the candies, fruit, and flowers to the gods during prayer. The priest takes our offerings, blesses them, and returns them to us to distribute. We call worshipping our gods puja.

Temple offerings are called prashad.

Brightly colored carvings of 72 gods and goddesses

Singapore's oldest Hindu temple, built in 1843

We offer candies and fruits to the gods

Puja tray

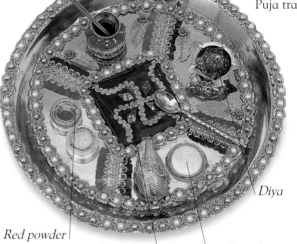

Red powder for tilak marks

Incense to purify the air

Milk and water to wash the gods

Diya

The priest in the temple helps us pray.

He prays on our behalf because he is wise and knows the religious texts. The priest uses these objects on a puja tray for temple worship. He also looks after the various gods. He washes their statues with milk and water.

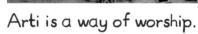

Arti is a way of worship.

All the Earth's elements—fire, water, earth, and air—are represented. Every day, many Hindus worship God in this way. After arti, everyone shares the prashad blessed by the gods.

India

My favorite god is Rama because he fought for my religion and won against evil Ravana. Believing in my religion is important to me so that is why I pray to Lord Rama. I have been to a temple that has a statue with Rama in it.

Sonam

My temple is white and pure-looking.

My mother and father take me there on special occasions. There are many gods there, all beautifully decorated. The incense sticks give off a lovely smell.

The four goals

KAMA, ARTHA, DHARMA, AND MOKSHA

MY NAME IS SHIVANI, after the god Shiva. At home we have a shrine to Shiva where we worship every day. I enjoy helping others, and when I leave school I'd like to be a nurse. My religion teaches me a lot about good and evil. I learn how important it is to obey rules, follow God's path, and to help and be good to others. Reaching for the four goals in my life helps me to be a caring, respectful person.

Shivani from Australia

Kama is about enjoying life.

I enjoy playing my guitar and dancing, especially Indian dancing. I also like making puri (fried circles of flat bread), and I have fun playing with sparklers at Divali.

It's important for Hindus to provide for their families.

The goal called Artha means working hard at school or at your job and being as successful as you can. Some children perform Artha by helping their parents with the family business. Others work hard to earn an allowance.

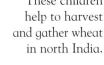

Indian rupee coins

These children help to harvest and gather wheat in north India.

Treating animals with respect is part of Dharma.

That's why so many Hindus are vegetarians. Caring for animals and treating them with kindness is important. Dharma is doing your duty toward God, your family, yourself, and others around you.

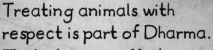

Vipul

US

Hinduism teaches you to do good things without expecting something in return. You learn to give value to friendships. If my friend needs help I will help him without thinking "please do me a favor also."

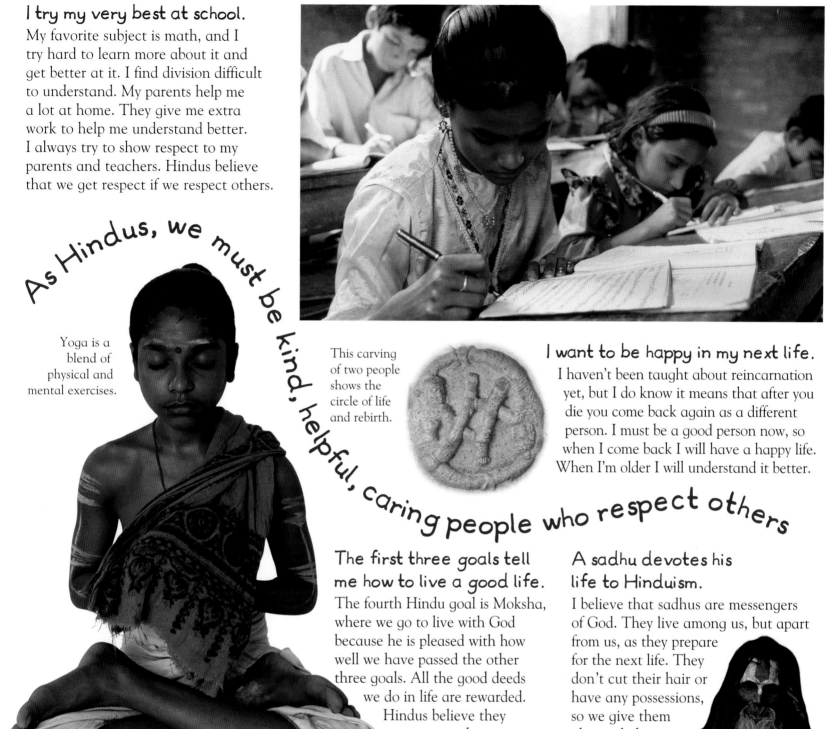

I try my very best at school.
My favorite subject is math, and I try hard to learn more about it and get better at it. I find division difficult to understand. My parents help me a lot at home. They give me extra work to help me understand better. I always try to show respect to my parents and teachers. Hindus believe that we get respect if we respect others.

As Hindus, we must be kind, helpful, caring people who respect others

Yoga is a blend of physical and mental exercises.

This carving of two people shows the circle of life and rebirth.

I want to be happy in my next life.
I haven't been taught about reincarnation yet, but I do know it means that after you die you come back again as a different person. I must be a good person now, so when I come back I will have a happy life. When I'm older I will understand it better.

The first three goals tell me how to live a good life.
The fourth Hindu goal is Moksha, where we go to live with God because he is pleased with how well we have passed the other three goals. All the good deeds we do in life are rewarded. Hindus believe they can come closer to finding Moksha through doing yoga.

A sadhu devotes his life to Hinduism.
I believe that sadhus are messengers of God. They live among us, but apart from us, as they prepare for the next life. They don't cut their hair or have any possessions, so we give them alms to help pay for their food and clothes.

India
I think good actions are that we should always tell the truth and never disobey our elders. We should help around the house. And we should eat our food on time and go out to play.

Adya

Anant

India
We should never tell a lie and we should always wash our hands before eating and bathe before going to sleep. And we should never eat food that has fallen on the floor.

Wedding

A HINDU MARRIAGE

I AM TRISHAL and I am 12. I love going to the beach and surfing the internet. I like being a Hindu because of the peaceful message of my faith. Hindu scriptures tell us that getting married and having a family is an important stage of life for all Hindus. This is why Hindu marriages are often arranged by the parents, who like to suggest a suitable partner for their son or daughter.

Trishal from Singapore

The bride wears a red and gold sari and lots of gold jewelry.

Before the wedding there is a Mehndi ceremony for the bride.
The wedding joins two families, as well as two people. The female relatives prepare by decorating the bride's hands with henna, a paste that leaves a red stain. The designs are called Mehndi.

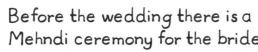

The bride and groom look amazing

Gifts are given.
The bride and groom welcome each other with garlands of fresh flowers. There are also gifts for other family members.

The groom arrives on a horse.
The horse wears a fancy blanket and saddle. A procession of wedding guests follows the groom. They can be very noisy. The bride's mother greets the groom and guides him to the canopy (mandapa) where the wedding takes place.

The groom and his male guests may wear turbans.

The bride and groom take their vows.

The priest leads the ceremony. There are prayers to the gods and special rituals. The bride and groom are joined by a white thread to show that they are married. Then they walk seven times around a sacred fire. Each circle they make represents one of seven prayers that they make for their life together. After that, they are husband and wife.

The priest ties a white thread to the bride and groom.

Purifying sacred fire

Flower petals signify beauty

Coconut is a fertility symbol.

Everyone in the family dresses up for this important occasion.

Boys sometimes wear turbans like the men. After the wedding we shower the couple with flowers and rice. Then we gather at the homes of the bride's and groom's parents for lots of food and fun.

Ganesh's image is placed in the corner of the mandapa.

When Hindus start something new, they usually pray to Ganesh, the god of good fortune. So he is always the most important god at a wedding ceremony.

Statue of Ganesh

Australia

As part of the wedding ceremony, the bride and groom take an oath in front of the fire to say that they will both live togther for the rest of their lives. The fire is a real fire.

Roja

US

I have not been to a Hindu wedding yet but hope that I will do this one day. I like the various Hindu festivals and my favorite is Divali. This is when we thank goddess Lakshmi and seek her blessing and protection.

Deepika

Buddhism

BUDDHISM IS NOT LIKE OTHER FAITHS. Its followers, who are called Buddhists, live according to the teachings of Buddha, its founder. Buddha did not believe in a supreme god, so Buddhists do not worship Buddha in that way. Instead, they pay respect to him and to all living beings. Buddha taught that life moves in an endless cycle of life, death, and rebirth. If people live with neither too much nor too little and are kind, they come closer to a joyful state of understanding called enlightenment. This is the goal of Buddhists.

Symbol

The Wheel of Dhamma (teaching) is the symbol of Buddhism. Buddhists believe that Buddha set this wheel of learning in motion. It also represents the cycle of life and rebirth.

Holy books

After Buddha died, his followers wrote his teachings down on palm leaves and placed the manuscripts in three baskets. These scriptures are known as the Tipitaka, or the Three Baskets.

Buddha's life

Buddha was born a prince in India about 500 BCE. One day he saw death, pain, and disease. He also saw a holy man who had achieved peace of mind. Buddha thought deeply about this until he became enlightened on how to live.

A hand gesture is called a mudra, which means "sign" or "symbol."

Buddha's hand gestures

In Buddhist art, the gestures Buddha makes with his hands have special meanings.

Statues of Buddha often show him with one hand raised, a gesture of blessing and fearlessness.

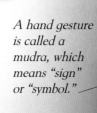

An open hand that points downward is an expression of generosity. Buddha teaches with an open hand.

Buddha's right hand touches the ground to remind Buddhists that the Earth is a witness to the truth.

Here Buddha's forefinger and thumb make the dhamma, or teaching, gesture.

How Buddhists worship

This young Burmese boy is visiting a shrine at a Buddhist temple. Buddhists visit monasteries or temples to think about Buddha and his teachings and to celebrate festivals. Buddhist homes often have a shrine with an image or statue of Buddha, surrounded by candles, flowers, small bells, bowls of water, or sticks of fragrant incense.

A place of pilgrimage

Buddhists believe that there are sacred places—buildings, mountains, or trees—that are worthy of a special visit. This temple is important to Buddhists because it was built in the exact spot where Buddha achieved enlightenment. The Mahabodhi temple is in Bodh Gaya, India. The main tower is 177 ft (54 m) tall, and its brick walls are decorated with beautiful carvings. A gigantic golden statue of the Buddha is housed inside.

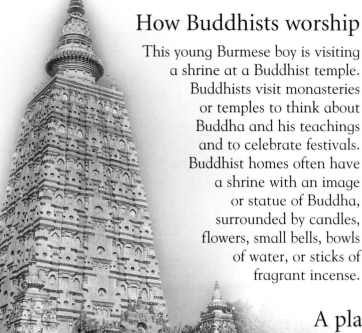

Schools of Buddhism

All Buddhists believe in the truth of Buddha's teachings, but different groups feel that there are separate paths to the truth. Theravada Buddhists are often encouraged to become monks and nuns and to follow Buddha's teachings as closely as possible. Mahayana Buddhists share the belief that anyone can become enlightened, without having to become a monk or a nun.

Tibetan Mahayana Buddhists use prayer wheels to spread blessings.

Theravada monks and nuns wear orange robes colored with plant dyes.

Rites of passage

Some Buddhist boys become novice monks, shaving their heads and living a simple life. Other Buddhists give food and support to monks to gain merit.

Main festivals

Parinirvana (Mahayana) Buddha's death *February*
Hana Matsuri (Mahayana) Buddha's birth *April*
Wesak (Theravada) Celebrates Buddha's birth, enlightenment, and death *April*
Obon (Mahayana) The story of Buddha *July*
Esala Perahera (Theravada) Festival of the Tooth *July/August*
Kathina (Theravada) Offerings are given to monasteries *October*
Nirvana Day (Mahayana) Buddha's enlightenment *December*

Where Buddhists live

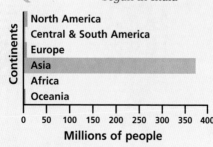

North America
Europe
Asia
Africa
Central & South America
Oceania

Buddhism began in India

Continents:
North America
Central & South America
Europe
Asia
Africa
Oceania

0 50 100 150 200 250 300 350 400
Millions of people

There are about 500 million followers of Buddhism throughout the world. The greatest number of Buddhists live in Asia, which is the region where Buddhism was founded.

Training to be a monk

LIVING ACCORDING TO BUDDHA'S TEACHINGS

MY NAME IS JANG-CHUB, and I am 11 years old. For the past year I have been living away from my family and friends as a novice monk. Being a novice means that I live and study at the Buddhist monastery, but I haven't yet taken my vows to stay forever. My father helped me to decide to become a novice when I was 10, but some children join when they are eight or nine. The thing I like best is learning the dhamma, Buddha's teachings.

Jang-chub from Tibet

At the monastery, everyone has his head shaved.

My friend does mine for me. We all wear the same clothes, too. In the outside world, clothes and hair can distract people from how they ought to live.

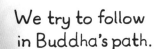

The dhamma is the most important thing to me

We try to follow in Buddha's path.

If a boy joins a monastery, it is a great honor for his family. Some boys are dressed in fancy clothes and paraded through the streets first. They enter the temple for a grand ceremony. Then they change into plain robes.

Alms bowl

Robes

Needle and thread

Razor

South Korea

I get up at 4 a.m. each day to worship the Buddha statue. I also study the scriptures and have learned to play the wooden drum while prayers are being recited. Sometimes we go on a picnic.

Seong-ho

We don't need much.

Everything we need is given to us. We wear plain red robes and flip-flops inside the monastery, and shoes outside. We have a razor to shave our heads, and a needle and thread to repair our robes. Some monks have alms bowls, but Tibetan monks don't.

Novices monks in Burma
receive alms from local people.

We eat simple food.

In some countries, Buddhists put gifts
of food in the monks' bowls. The money to
buy our food is donated at the temple. At
breakfast we have Tibetan tea with butter, bread, and
potato curry. Lunch is dhal (lentil soup), rice, vegetables,
and meat. Dinner is the same, but maybe with noodles.

We should be kind to all creatures.

There are three dogs,
one parrot, four fish, and
a crow to look after at
my monastery. A monk's
religious training teaches
him not to harm or kill
any living beings. We are
also taught not to
steal, tell lies,
get married, or
behave badly.
It's easy to
remember.

This novice in
Burma cares
for a puppy.

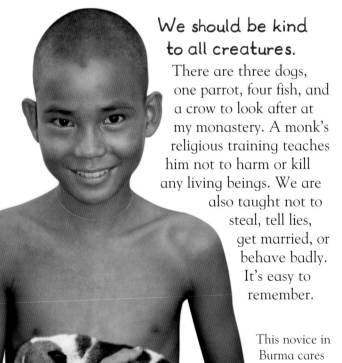

I love learning at the monastery.

We wake up at sunrise and have a Nepali
class for one hour. After breakfast, we
read Tibetan texts. We study Tibetan
writing before tea. If we miss a class,
we have to pay 25 rupees (60 cents).

I enjoy my free time.

Before lunch and after tea, I
have time for myself. Sometimes
I study, but I like to play games,
too. Sunday is the only day I
can leave the monastery to visit
my family and see my friends.

Wesak

BUDDHA DAY

I'M JEFFREY, and I'm eight years old. One day I would like to be a dentist and a pianist. My favorite hobby is playing chess. When my brother was alive, he used to play games with me. He taught me to keep trying and never to give up. Now I am learning to be brave like my brother. I go to the temple a few times a year. I like the chanting songs. I feel happy when I hear them. My favorite celebration is Wesak. It is the day that we celebrate the birth of Buddha.

Jeffrey from Canada

Everyone tries to be kind.

We make lanterns and send greeting cards to each other and everyone is happy. The Buddha taught us not to harm other living creatures and to love everyone. It is good to be a vegetarian for a day on Wesak to remember that Buddha cared for all creatures.

I help bathe the Buddha to get his blessing

On Wesak, my mom buys flowers and fruits.

These are for our prayer offering at the temple. The temple is so crowded. People leave their offerings by the statue. I bow to Buddha and remember my brother as I chant and meditate.

We hang up lanterns.

All around the world, Buddhists decorate temples and trees with lanterns and lights. The lights help us to think about Buddha's enlightenment. In some places, Buddhists parade through the streets holding lighted candles.

We bathe the Buddha.

At the temple, I help to wash the small statues of Buddha as a child. These are often scattered with flower petals. The monk gives away blessing strings as a birthday gift. If we tie the string around our wrists, it will bring us good luck.

Flowers like this lotus blossom are offered to Buddha.

Hana Matsuri

Buddhists in Japan celebrate Buddha's birthday at Hana Matsuri, a flower festival. Children make paper flowers to remind them of the beautiful gardens where Buddha was born. They dress in their best clothes and walk beside floats full of flowers in a parade to the temple . Everyone throws lotus flowers into the path of the procession.

At night, we parade with our lanterns.

It's called a light parade. We also have lanterns when we celebrate the Moon festival. Children are allowed to stay up late. We play with lanterns until the full Moon rises. Some people pray to the Moon because they believe an angel lives up there.

Suzzane

Borneo

On Wesak I gave the Buddha a bath. The monk distributed flowers, and we used them in the bath. The scent of flowers is nice.

Leanne Son

Australia

I go to the Cambodian temple to pray on special occasions, We prepare food and serve it to the monks, who say prayers to the gods and ancestors.

Ways of worship

DEVOTION TO BUDDHA

HELLO, MY NAME IS MAIKO. I enjoy listening to pop music and walking our family dog. So far, I have traveled to Germany and Australia. I dream of visiting more places, and meeting people on the way. I live in a temple because both my parents work as priests. My father began to teach me how to recite a sutra (scripture) called the O-kyo when I was three years old. Buddhism teaches us to be aware of ourselves, and to review our attitudes again and again.

Maiko from Japan

Buddhists spend time chanting at home.
I feel calm and softened when we recite the O-kyo sutra at home. For us, it is very important to do this.

A nun in Scotland sits at her bedroom shrine.

We recite the O-kyo using prayer beads.
As we recite the sutra, our fingers move from one bead to the next. Most juzu have 108 beads.

Each bead represents a desire that must be overcome.

My religion has always been with me

Our temple is also my home.
The main building in the middle of the temple complex is called the hondo. At the heart of the hondo is my favorite place in the temple, the Amida-sama, or Buddha statue. I feel very calm when I sit there.

Outside the temple is a gong.
It is struck 10 times every day, at sunset and during religious celebrations. I'm very fond of striking it, since I've done it since I was small.

Hoang

Vietnam
I go with my mom and dad to my grandad's grave. I light the incense and pray to Buddha to look after grandad in Heaven. I hope Buddha hears me.

Zoe

US
Buddhism is very peaceful. My brother and I chant to overcome challenges. We also chant for the happiness of others. When friends ask what the altar is, I say it's where we pray.

Rice and lotus flower temple offering

Some Buddhists fly prayer flags.

When the wind blows, the prayer flags flutter and carry blessings for goodness, healing, and happiness through the breeze to everyone in the world.

We thank Buddha by making offerings.

People don't have to give money. Working for the temple or spreading his teaching is also important.

Buddha watches us and cares for us.

In the temple, we sit on tatami mats that cover the floor. We all follow my father's instructions because he is the chief priest. We light candles as we recite the O-kyo to show our respect, and we burn incense to purify ourselves.

Esala Perahera

FESTIVAL OF THE TOOTH

MY NAME IS HASINI. I am 10 years old, and my favorite hobby is collecting stamps and stickers. I like reading books, and when I graduate I want to be a scientist. Once or twice a week I visit the temple. It is built of white-washed plaster, with high steps leading up to a Buddha statue. Every year, we celebrate a festival in honor of Buddha's tooth.

Hasini from Sri Lanka

The elephants walk along so slowly and proudly

I have seen Buddha's tooth twice.

His tooth is very brown and about 1½ in (4 cm) long. It sits on a velvet base covered by a glass bowl. The tooth is so precious that a temple was built here in Kandy to house it. During the festival, the tooth is paraded in a casket on an elephant's back.

The Raja—a very large elephant—carries the sacred tooth under a canopy.

The casket is made of gold and studded with gems.

Inside the Temple of the Tooth

First, we have the Kap ceremony.

The night before the festival starts, a branch of a jackfruit tree that has never borne fruit is planted near the temple. Then the festival can begin.

This girl is holding up a jackfruit.

Sri Lanka

The procession is very short at the beginning of the festival. Every day it gets longer and longer as more elephants join in. They are covered in tiny lightbulbs at night. Last time, I saw about 113 elephants, and two baby elephants as well. I like the dancers best.

Dilrupa

The sights and sounds at night are so exciting.

The first sound you hear is the whip crackers, then the parades begin. There are drummers, dancers, stilt walkers, somersaulters, and singers. I have also seen the colorful floats of the gods. Everything sparkles with gold and jewels. I have fun with my family, especially my cousins, who are all my age. We watch everything together.

The dancers that follow the elephants have the brightest costumes.

One year I counted 55 elephants.

I usually watch the parades from the balcony of a friend's store. The elephants are one of the best parts. They are always dressed in rich, dark colors, with each color representing a different god. Sometimes the elephants are sprinkled with gold dust. The festival lasts for two weeks.

Drummer playing a thammattama drum

Fire-eaters carry lighted torches.

Symbol

The Khanda is made up of several symbols. At the center is a double-edged sword that represents the divine power of God. The circle shows that God has no beginning and no end. Two crossed swords (called kirpan) represent a Sikh's responsibility to God and to the community.

Holy book

The collection of Sikh holy verses is called the Guru Granth Sahib. Sikhs believe that this book is the living word of God and show respect by waving a chauri (animal-hair fan) over it when it is read.

Guru Granth Sahib and chauri

Guru Nanak

Sikhism

THE BEAUTIFUL GOLDEN TEMPLE, sacred to the faith of Sikhism, has a door on each of its four sides to show that it is open to people from all four corners of the globe. In the same way, Sikhism grew as a faith open to one and all, in which everyone is equal in the eyes of the one true God. Sikhism (Sikh means "disciple" or "student") is only 500 years old, and the religion is built on the ideas of its founder, the Guru Nanak.

How Sikhs worship

Sikhs pray to God daily. They worship with other Sikhs in a building called a gurdwara. A Sikh service includes prayers, readings from the Guru Granth Sahib, and hymns (called kirtan), accompanied by musical instruments such as sitars and drums.

Sitar

Drawing closer to God

These children enjoy a dip in the waters surrounding the Golden Temple in the Punjab, northern India. This is one of the most important and famous Sikh holy places, and many people try to visit it. Sikhs believe that God reaches out through the teachings of the Guru Granth Sahib. In return, they can come closer to God by worshipping God and serving the Sikh community.

Founder of the faith

The Sikh religion was founded by Guru Nanak (1469–1539). Guru is the name for a spiritual teacher. Born near Lahore (now in Pakistan), Nanak was brought up a Hindu, but had an idea for a new religion. His most important teachings were that everyone has access to the one true God without special rituals or priests, and that everyone is equal in God's eyes.

The Ten Gurus

Before Nanak died, he appointed a new leader. In all, nine men were named Guru after Nanak (the largest face on this poster). The holy book, the Guru Granth Sahib, is now regarded as the main guru of Sikhism.

Performing seva

Sikhs try to do good in the world and help other people, a duty called seva. Many Sikhs do chores at the gurdwara, from cleaning up to helping cook and serve a community meal. Sikhs must also give money to charity and care for the needy.

Rites of passage

Every Sikh baby has a naming ceremony. The Guru Granth Sahib is opened at random and the first letter of the reading becomes the first letter of the child's name. The baby is also given a steel bracelet to wear as a sign of his or her faith. Older children may choose to enter the Khalsa, a committed group of Sikhs.

Where Sikhs live

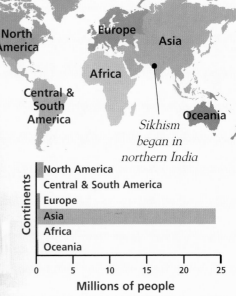

Sikhism began in northern India

Most Sikhs live in the Punjab, a region that includes parts of Pakistan and India. There are about a million Sikhs who live outside the Punjab in places such as Canada, the United States, and the United Kingdom.

Main festivals

Guru Gobind Singh's birthday *January*
Hola Mohalla Festival of martial arts *February/March*
Baisakhi Celebrates the founding of the Khalsa and Sikhism *March/April*
Martyrdom of Guru Arjan *June*
Divali Celebrates Guru Hargobind's release from prison *October/November*
Guru Nanak's birthday *November*
Martyrdom of Guru Tegh Bahadur *December/January*

Day at the gurdwara

SIKH PLACE OF WORSHIP

MY NAME IS VIJAYANT and I'm 14 years old. My favorite hobbies include computers, playing tennis and cricket, and surfing. After I finish school I hope to go to law school and become a lawyer. I like belonging to a Sikh community, and I think it is important to set aside a day to worship together. My parents and I visit our gurdwara once a month, and for special celebrations. I love the peaceful atmosphere there, and the day is always special.

Vijayant from Australia

Gurdwara means "home for the Guru."

My gurdwara has a big dome and a hall where services take place. It is decorated with paintings of the gurus and special religious stories. There is also a langar where we sit down to eat a meal.

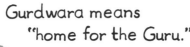

We have to take our shoes off before going inside.

We also have to cover our heads. This is a sign of respect. There is usually someone looking after the shoes while people are inside. It is a way of performing seva (serving others).

I enjoy the music and singing.

For most of the service people sing prayers, called kirtan, from the Guru Granth Sahib. I haven't learned the words yet. At my gurdwara, musicians play tabla (drums) and harmonium (a reed organ). I would like to play the harmonium because it has an uplifting sound.

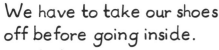

Everyone sits on the floor so that they are all equal. The Guru Granth Sahib rests on a cushion on a raised platform in front of everyone. It is carried into the main hall in the morning and it is treated with great respect. The first thing I do is walk up to the platform and bow down. Then I make money offerings. Throughout the service, the holy book is fanned very slowly and elegantly with a chauri. At the end of the day the Guru Granth Sahib is taken back to its special resting place.

Belonging to a community helps me to feel a closeness to God

We eat our meals together.
First we share a sacred pudding—called prashad—that is blessed at the end of the service. I like the taste. Then we sit down in the langar where a vegetarian meal is served to everyone. Many people help to prepare and serve the food. I like the roti and dhal best.

Some children go to school at the gurdwara.
Girls and boys learn to read the Guru Granth Sahib. I would like to know more about the history of Sikhism.

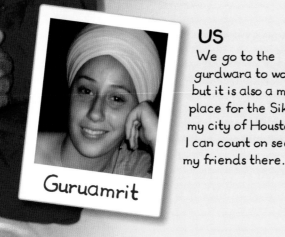

US
We go to the gurdwara to worship, but it is also a meeting place for the Sikhs in my city of Houston. I can count on seeing my friends there.

Guruamrit

UK
When I go to the gurdwara there is a big flag and we pray to it. There is a man who waves a stick with the guru's hair. We give money and we get prashad to eat. We use a tissue to wipe our hands afterward.

Malkeet

Baisakhi

FESTIVAL OF THE FOUNDING OF THE KHALSA

MY NAME IS SHEETAL, and I am nine years old. I have one brother and one sister, and I would like to be a teacher when I grow up. The most memorable day of my life so far was when I visited the Golden Temple in Amritsar. I cannot describe the feelings I had that day. I try to remember that feeling on Baisakhi, the spring festival that celebrates the founding of the Khalsa.

Sheetal from the UK

It's quite a thrill to watch the sword fights and street parades

The Five Beloved were the first members of the Khalsa.

The Khalsa was founded by the tenth guru, Gobind Singh. He asked who would give his life for the Sikh faith. Five men stepped forward. They were called the Five Beloved, the faithful ones.

Samosas

In the morning we lower the old flag at the gurdwara.

We wash the pole and then raise the new flag. This marks the start of the Sikh New Year. Almost everyone helps.

I like to eat samosas.

During the mela, or street fair, food stalls offer all kinds of snacks from the Punjab area of India.

When the flag pole is lowered, many people wash it with milk, or with yogurt and water.

The Nagar Kirtan is a street parade.

It starts and ends at the gurdwara and is led by drummers beating traditional Punjabi drums. Next come men playing gatka, a traditional martial art. I like watching the men swing their swords in mock fights. Everyone sings and follows the parade.

The Guru Granth Sahib is carried through the streets.

The holy book is part of the procession at many festivals. It rests on cushions that are placed on a throne, called Palki Sahib. The throne is draped in white sheets and carried under a canopy covered in beautiful flowers. Some people who carry the Guru Granth Sahib wear blue turbans or sashes, like those worn by the Five Beloved over their yellow robes.

Orange and blue balloons add to the color of the festival.

It's fun to be part of the mela.

Last Baisakhi, my cousins and I went together. There were 20 of us in all, and we were allowed to stay up late because it wasn't a school night. I enjoyed watching the Bhangra dancers perform in their amazing clothes and turbans.

India

At Baisakhi we go to the temple and have food called lungha. We pray and give money for charity. I used to wear my hair long, but the tightness made my head sore and I decided to cut my hair.

Prithvi

Joining the Khalsa

A SPECIAL COMMUNITY OF SIKHS

MY NAME IS BHAVKEERAT and I'm 14. My hobbies are music and cycling. I go to high school in Amritsar, the city of the Golden Temple. I study Sikhism and other subjects at school, and when I'm older I want to be a doctor, like my parents. I go to my gurdwara almost every day. I enjoy listening to the kirtan, eating the prashad, and helping out with the langar. In my faith, it is considered a matter of great privilege to join the Khalsa at a special ceremony.

Bhavkeerat from the Punjab

Kangha comb

Kaccha underpants

The five Ks show our faith.

Members who join the Khalsa wear five items that begin with the letter "K." Kesh is uncut hair, a symbol of listening to God's will. The kangha comb is for cleanliness. The kaccha (underpants) shows restraint. The kirpan isn't a weapon, but stands for justice. The kara, a steel bangle, shows God's unending strength.

Kirpan sword

Kara bracelet

Most Sikhs wear a turban.

A turban is a long piece of cloth that is wrapped around the head and tied. Members of the Khalsa must not cut their hair, so a turban keeps the hair clean and out of the way. It also shows respect for Guru Gobind Singh, who founded the Khalsa. When I go swimming, I just wear a patka.

1. The hair is put in a bun with the kangha, and then covered by a small cloth called a patka.

2. The long turban cloth is wound round and round the head, until just a little bit of turban remains.

3. The remaining loose end is tied and tucked in. Some people add a badge of the khanda symbol.

Five Khalsa members lead the amrit ceremony.

They are called the panj piares and represent the Five Beloved. The panj piares talk to the disciples about the duties of a Sikh. Then they use a sword to stir water and sugar in a batta (iron bowl) to make the amrit drink. The five men offer five sips of amrit to each person who wants to join the Khalsa.

Anyone who wants to join the Khalsa should sit down in the presence of the Guru Granth Sahib to offer prayers and drink amrit.

Wearing the five Ks is the most important thing

You have to feel ready to join.

I think I will join the Khalsa a little later in life, when I have completed my school studies. I have talked with my grandparents about this, and they have the same feeling. They joined a few years ago. Girls as well as boys can join.

These nervous young boys, who are about to join the Khalsa, are wearing the five Ks. They wear patkas over their uncut hair.

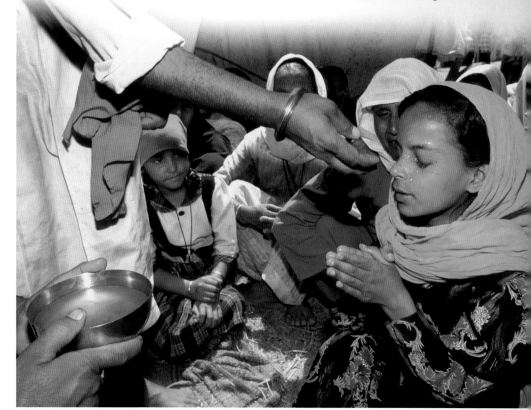

UK

Joining the Khalsa is extremely important. I have kept my hair long my whole life and I plan on keeping long hair for the rest of my life. I am very serious about my religion and go to Punjabi school twice a week.

Jasdip

Amrit is sprinkled over the eyes and head of the disciple.

The panj piares do this to each person joining the Khalsa, as he or she chants a religious verse. Then everyone is asked to drink amrit from the same batta. There is no special music or blessing to welcome new members into the community. At the end of the ceremony everyone shares a little of the sweet food, called prashad.

Hola Mohalla

A FESTIVAL OF MOCK BATTLES

I'M GURKARAN and I'm 12 years old. My favorite hobby is meteorology. That's the science of weather. I like being a Sikh because my religion discourages discrimination and encourages me to help people, especially needy people. My faith also makes me feel that I'm different and that I stand out. In the past, Sikhs have died for their faith. Every year, we have a festival to celebrate how much Sikhs care about defending their religion.

Nihang shield

Gurkaran from India

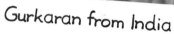

Long sword

There were some special weapons.

I saw a long, thin spear. It was probably about 10 ft (3 m) long. The performers who used these kinds of weapons at the festival didn't hit each other's swords and sticks much, but when they did you could hear an echo around the stadium.

The horses and riders were amazing!

Hola Mohalla began in 1700.

The tenth guru, Guru Gobind Singh, had many reasons for starting the festival. Hola Mohalla showed people that the Khalsa were prepared to go to war to defend their right to believe in their faith. The new festival also gave Sikhs an alternative to Holi (the Hindu festival), which is about playing practical jokes.

I watched some mock battles.

Everybody wanted to see the Nihang Sikhs stage their Gatka (mock battles). Nihang is a Persian word meaning "crocodile." The Nihangs are voluntary Sikh soldiers. Many of them carry guns, various types of swords and spears, and some even have bows and arrows. They wear large turbans that are decorated with steel rings, called chakkars.

There were horses galloping all around the stadium.

Some of the horses had drums on their backs that were being beaten ferociously. The crowds really liked the performers who stood up on two galloping horses. I was surprised that none of them fell off.

Amandeep

UK

It's not a festival that we celebrate here. But my family comes from the Punjab, where it is known as the Festival of Nihangs. These were brave warrior Sikhs who defended the Sikh way of life during times of persecution.

There is a langar every day.

I generally help at the langar meal in the gurdwara by cooking rotis, serving food, and washing dishes. But this was our first time at Hola Mohalla, so we did not help. I ate some dhal and roti. My favorite treat was a special candy called jalabee.

The festival is full of color.

Nihangs wear dark blue knee-length kurtas and orange sashes. We throw colored powder too, so people are covered in color.

Symbol

The Star of David is most commonly linked with Judaism today. It is in the shape of King David's shield. In the Hebrew Bible, David (who had great faith in God) was a hero because he killed the giant Goliath.

Judaism

FOLLOWERS OF JUDAISM worship one God, and they are all the children of Abraham, the man who brought God's message to the people. The holy book of Judaism, the Torah, tells the story of how God promised to protect Abraham's people if they vowed to love and obey God, and to follow God's laws. The most important laws are the Ten Commandments, handed down from God to a leader named Moses.

Holy book

The story of how the Jewish faith began is told in the Torah. The Torah, which means "law," is the first five books of the Hebrew Bible. It contains rules for daily life and for worship and is printed on a long scroll.

Mezuzah

Many Jews affix a small box, called a mezuzah, to the front doors of their homes. Inside is a tiny scroll with a special prayer, called the Shema, honoring God.

Father of the faith

Abraham lived in what is now Iraq more than 4,000 years ago. In his day, people worshipped different gods. But Abraham believed there was only one God, who would look after people forever if they obeyed God's laws. This is why Jews became known as God's chosen people.

Moses and the Ten Commandments

Moses

The Torah tells the story of Moses, who was a leader of the Jews. God gave Moses the Ten Commandments (a set of rules for people to follow) on two stone tablets.

1	I am the only God. Worship no god but me.
2	Do not make idols of images of God to worship.
3	Respect God's name.
4	Keep the Sabbath (day of rest) holy.
5	Respect your father and mother.
6	Do not kill.
7	Do not be unfaithful to your husband or wife.
8	Do not steal.
9	Do not tell lies about other people.
10	Do not envy the things that other people have.

Praying to God

Prayer is central to Judaism. Many Jews pray three times a day, as well as in the morning and at night. Some Jews wear a tallit, or prayer shawl (above), over their heads when they pray, or at ceremonies.

A scattered nation

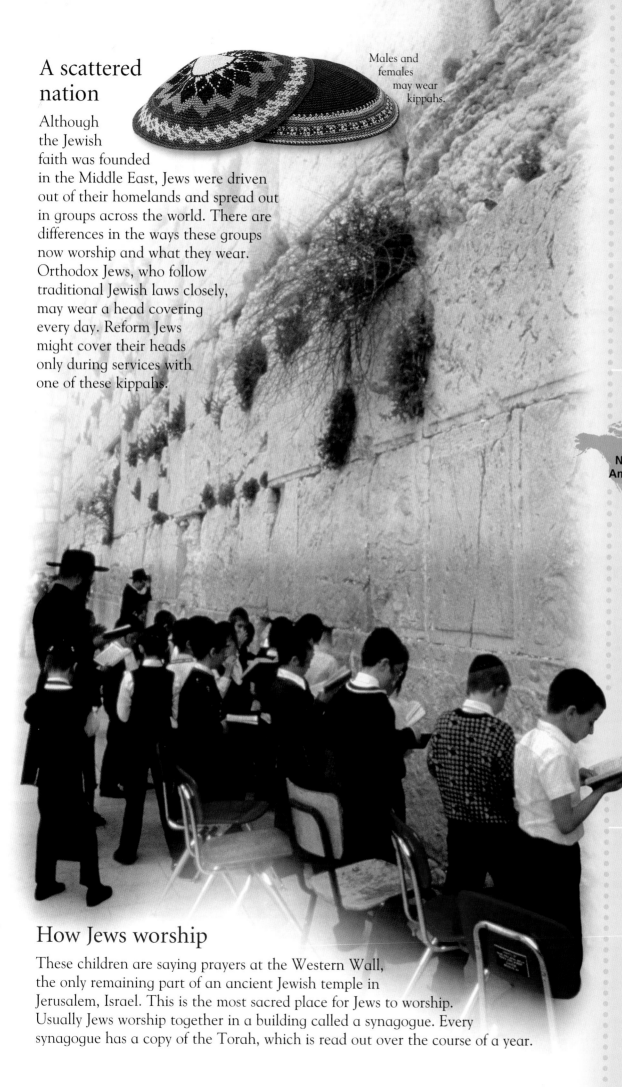

Males and females may wear kippahs.

Although the Jewish faith was founded in the Middle East, Jews were driven out of their homelands and spread out in groups across the world. There are differences in the ways these groups now worship and what they wear. Orthodox Jews, who follow traditional Jewish laws closely, may wear a head covering every day. Reform Jews might cover their heads only during services with one of these kippahs.

How Jews worship

These children are saying prayers at the Western Wall, the only remaining part of an ancient Jewish temple in Jerusalem, Israel. This is the most sacred place for Jews to worship. Usually Jews worship together in a building called a synagogue. Every synagogue has a copy of the Torah, which is read out over the course of a year.

Rites of passage

Jewish children are born into their faith. Jewish boys are circumcized eight days after birth (below) and given a Jewish name. Girls are also named and blessed. Children officially join the synagogue at a bar mitzvah (boys) or bat mitzvah (girls) ceremony.

Where Jews live

North America

Europe

Asia

Africa

Central & South America

Oceania

Judaism began in Israel

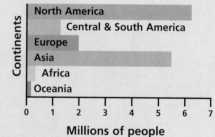

North America

Central & South America

Europe

Asia

Africa

Oceania

Continents

0 1 2 3 4 5 6 7

Millions of people

The largest populations of Jews in the world are in North America (where more than six million Jews live) and in Asia, home to more than five million Jews (mainly in Israel).

Main festivals

Shabbat Day of rest and worship from Friday night to Saturday night *weekly*

Purim Celebrates the bravery of Queen Esther *February/March*

Passover Remembers the deliverance from slavery in Egypt *March/April*

Rosh Hashanah New Year's Day *October*

Yom Kippur Day of repentance *October*

Hanukkah Festival of lights *December*

Passover

AN EIGHT-DAY FESTIVAL

MY NAME IS YAEL, and I am almost 11 years old. I have two brothers and a sister. When I grow up I want to be an actress. We walk to the Orthodox synagogue every Saturday. I enjoy saying the Shema because I know it so well. Passover is a festival that reminds us of the story of the Jewish people who were taken out of Egypt from slavery to freedom.

Yael from Israel

At the Seder all the family is together

Egg symbolizes biblical sacrifices

Vegetable representing spring

Lamb shank

Charoset paste

Bitter root

The Seder is the most important meal.

We eat special foods that symbolize Passover. Bitter root reminds us of the bitter lives of the slaves. We dip potato in salty water to remember the tears they shed. We mix dates, apples, and nuts to make charoset, like the cement the slaves made to build the pharaoh's cities. We eat lamb to remember God's plague passing over the homes marked with lambs' blood.

We get rid of all the chametz in the house.

During Passover, we don't eat chametz (bread and foods made with yeast). The evening before Seder, my father lights a candle to look for any crumbs, and we follow. He asks us if we are sure we have removed all the chametz.

The house is cleaned top to bottom.

Getting rid of every trace of chametz is a lot of work. I cleaned my room, vacuumed the rug, and dusted my toys, books, and clothes so well that there were no crumbs in them. Then I helped get out our special Passover dishes.

Argentina

At Passover we have lots of special foods and a big family meal that's called a Seder. I love eating the matzoh because they are crispy. The bitter root tastes horrid though.

Dan

The youngest child may sing the questions.

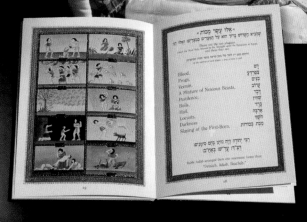

The *Haggadah* explains the story of how God helped the Jews to escape from Egypt.

We eat a special yeastless bread called matzoh.

This is to remind us of when the Jewish slaves left Egypt in a hurry, and their bread had no time to rise. My father breaks a matzoh in two and hides one half. We try to find it and hide it somewhere else.

Matzoh crackers

We send cards to family and friends who miss our Seder.

We gather at my grandfather's house for the Seder on the first night of Passover. There are prayers in the synagogue, but Passover is mainly celebrated at home.

At the Seder, we tell the story of Passover.

This is called the *Haggadah*. My family and I sit at the table and listen to the words that remind us of the struggle of the past. It's tradition for the youngest child to ask set questions about why this night is different from all other nights of the year.

Festival of Purim

Esther was a Jewish queen who risked her own life to save the Jewish people from a villain called Haman. At Purim, Jewish families listen to the *Megillah* (the Book of Esther) at the synagogue. People exchange gifts, eat homentash, a special type of Purim cracker, and join parades wearing costumes.

When Haman's name is mentioned, people hiss or shake rattles.

Rattle

Hanukkah

A FESTIVAL OF LIGHTS

I'M BENJAMIN and I'm nine. I like using my imagination to pretend that I am an adventurer who has to escape from an enemy. My faith allows me to get in touch with my soul. I go to a traditional synagogue in a beautiful square in Paris. Every Sunday I study the Torah there. It's really interesting. During the festival of Hanukkah, we remember a special miracle that happened a long time ago.

Benjamin from France

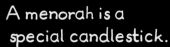
Roman oil lamp

A menorah is a special candlestick.
It holds eight candles for every day of the miracle, plus a chamach (candle). This last candle is used to light the others. My mom lights the chamach, then my brother and I light the other candles with the chamach, one more candle every day until the end of Hanukkah. We use a menorah from Israel.

We celebrate the miracle of the oil.
After the Jews defeated a cruel king about 2,000 years ago, the oil in their temple lamp burned for eight days instead of one.

Australia
In Australia Hanukkah time is hot and sunny. The days are long so we wait until 9 p.m. to light the big Hanukkiah in the park. This year my dad did the blessings, then we sang and danced and ate yummy foods.

Romi

Rachel

South Africa
We all light a menorah in our family. My sister and I light the menorahs that we made in school. I like playing games with the dreidl. I love to eat doughnuts and also potato latkes.

Some people use menorahs that have been in their families a long time.

Golden foil covers the gelt, or chocolate coins.

Spinning top called a dreidel

We play a game using a dreidel.

Each of its four sides is marked with the first initial from a Hebrew phrase, "Ness Gadol Haya Po" ("There was here a great miracle."). Chocolate coins can be used as a kitty. Each player spins the dreidel. If it lands on Ness, a player doesn't win or lose. For Gadol, a player takes all but one coin, and everyone puts a coin in the kitty. For Haya, a player takes half the kitty and, for Po, a player gives away a coin.

My soul is a sort of little ghost inside me

When a player has collected all the coins, he or she wins the dreidel game.

Every morning we exchange gifts.

We do this just after we wake up. My favorite present last year was some cards from my mother. We don't celebrate Hanukkah at school because it is not a Jewish school. I usually do some Hanukkah drawings with my Jewish friends, and we exchange small gifts. I also receive Happy Hanukkah cards and messages through email. Friends and family attach photos to their greetings.

Hanukkah gift

ברכות לחנוכה
Happy Hanukkah

HAPPY HANUKKAH
חג חנוכה שמח
HANUKKAH

Greeting cards

Jam doughnuts

We eat foods cooked in oil.

This is to remember the miracle of the lamp oil. My favorite food is doughnuts. My grandmother usually makes the food, but if she is not there during Hanukkah, my mother does the cooking. I set the table and put out prayer books.

Latkes (potato pancakes) being fried in oil

Simchat Torah

My favorite religious celebration is the Simchat Torah, because at this festival we start to reread the Torah. I have always understood that the Torah is the book of life. My family and I go to the synagogue to pray. During Simchat Torah we sing and dance around the holy book inside the synagogue.

Everyone is encouraged to carry the Torah. It is so heavy that children often carry miniature versions instead.

Bat Mitzvah

COMING OF AGE IN THE JEWISH FAITH

MY NAME IS ERIN, and I am 13 years old. I like to hang out with my friends or go on the internet to talk to them. Fridays are my favorite nights. Other nights of the week are a little crazy for my family, but on Shabbat we all sit down for a nice meal. We light candles and ask for God's blessing. My faith in God helps me heal my problems and answer my questions. This year, I had my Bat Mitzvah. I wanted people to see me for who I am, and my dedication to becoming a Jewish adult.

Erin from the US

Mitzvah class in Tel Aviv, Israel

We learn verses from the Torah at Hebrew school.

The Bat Mitzvah ceremony welcomes girls into the adult congregation. A mentor may help with the religious preparation. A few weeks before my Bat Mitzvah I discussed my Torah speech with my rabbi, and he helped me with it.

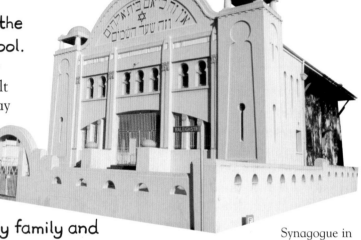

Synagogue in Port Elizabeth, South Africa

My family and friends filled the synagogue.

When I stood up on the Bimah and looked at them all, I remembered how everyone had helped me to reach where I am as a person and as a Jew. I designed my own tallit (prayer shawl) and helped to plan everything.

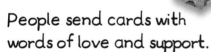

Girls may be showered with candies for a sweet life

I read from the Torah as part of the ceremony.

The scroll is heavy, and I was terrified I was going to drop it. The Torah was handed from my grandparents to my parents to me. I felt that I was part of a powerful tradition.

This girl reads from the Torah during her Bat Mitzvah.

I am now accepted as an adult

People send cards with words of love and support.

The messages in the cards are inspirational, because Bat Mizvah is an important stage in a girl's life.

After my ceremony, everyone shared a special prayer blessing.
The prayer is called the Kiddush, and it is said before breaking bread and drinking wine. I was also able to honor my family and some of my teachers by giving them an aliyah (a blessing over the Torah). It is one of the greatest honors a Jewish person can receive.

Challah bread

Kiddush cup

Bar Mitzvah

A boy joins the adult congregation at a Bar Mitzvah. He is then able to join in religious ceremonies. At many synagogues the service is the same as a Bat Mitzvah. A boy reads a section from the Torah and gives a speech.

Iraq
I am going to have my Bar Mitzvah when I am 13. It is a very special time. When I have my Bar Mitzvah I will read from the Torah. It is very hard to learn to read from the Torah. I may have my Bar Mitzvah in Israel, like my brother.

Ethan

Naomi

Romania
Bat Mitzvah is when a Jewish girl becomes responsible for her actions. I hope I will put a lot of effort into fulfilling as many good deeds as I can.

That night I had a party at a hotel in Hollywood to celebrate.
Some girls have a candle-lighting ceremony to honor family and friends. We had a havdala ceremony to mark the end of the Sabbath. After that, we danced the hora, a traditional Jewish folk dance. I was raised up above the dancers in a chair by four strong men. One of them was my 15-year-old brother!

Wedding celebration

A JEWISH MARRIAGE CEREMONY

I AM LIBBI, and I am nine years old. I love reading and cooking. I make latkes (potato pancakes) for Hanukkah, and challah (braided bread) for Shabbat. When I leave school I want to run a farm. My family and I go to the synagogue every Saturday morning. I particularly like our children's service on Saturdays. I went to the wedding of my Jewish friends, Mandy and Jason, recently. It was an important religious event, as well as a happy occasion.

Libbi from the UK

The groom's duties are written in the ketubah.
This is a marriage contract, and the groom signs it before the wedding. It is often written in beautiful handwriting. I saw it displayed on a table.

Ketubah

The service was held under a canopy.
It's called a huppah. It's a piece of cloth on four poles that is normally white and can have flowers on it. The huppah is a symbol of a couple's new home. Mandy wore a beautiful dress. She walked around Jason seven times to show that she is making a home with him.

The bride and groom gave each other rings.
They said vows to promise themselves to each other, and blessings were recited. It is a serious part of the ceremony. Mandy didn't wear any other jewellery.

Italian Jewish wedding ring

Sometimes the couple stands under a tallit.

This is instead of a huppah. As the wedding ceremony ends, the rabbi blesses the new husband and wife. He thanks God for creating human life and wishes the couple a long, healthy, and happy life together.

Traditional Jewish tallit, or prayer shawl

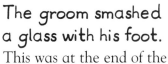

The groom smashed a glass with his foot.

This was at the end of the ceremony. Jason wrapped the glass in a cloth and stepped on it. There was a loud crunching sound! It is a Jewish tradition that reminds us that all happy occasions also have some sadness. Then everyone shouts out "Mazel Tov!" (Good Luck).

Everyone shouted "Mazel Tov!"

There was a big party after the wedding ceremony.

The wedding guests joined the new husband and wife to celebrate. I wore a pretty dress like the one I wear for Shabbat every week. My Dad wore his rabbi clothes. The women danced with the women, and the men danced together because this is a Jewish tradition. There was lots of chocolate to eat.

The bride and groom were lifted above our heads.

This was during the traditional circle dance, called a hora. The bride and groom sit in chairs, or on a board, and are lifted above the heads of all the dancers. This is to make them feel happy. They are like a king and queen for the day.

Yemen

Before the wedding, Yemenite Jews have a special celebration called a chinah. The bride wears a heavy headdress covered in jewels, and lots of rings on her fingers. She also has henna designs painted on her hands.

Nadav

Symbol

The symbol of the cross helps Christians to remember Christ's sacrifice by dying on a cross. But the image of an empty cross is perhaps an even stronger symbol, reminding Christians that Jesus came alive again to show that he was God's son, before ascending back up to heaven. Another popular symbol of early Christianity was a fish (below).

Holy book

The Bible contains the Old and New Testaments. (Testament means "promise".) What Christians call the Old Testament is also sacred to Jews and Muslims. The New Testament tells the story of Christ's life and teachings, his death and return to heaven, and the growth of early Christianity.

Christianity

TWO THOUSAND YEARS AGO in Israel, a great teacher spread a simple message: people must live God's word every day through acts of kindness and love. This man was Jesus Christ, whom Christians believe is God's son. Although Jesus inspired many people, he was put to death by the Romans, who ruled the area. Yet three days later Jesus rose from the dead. His life and teachings are celebrated in Christianity.

God's son

Christians believe that God sent Jesus to live on earth to tell people about God's love for them. They also believe that God allowed Jesus to die as a sacrifice to forgive the wrong things people do, and give people "new life", or a fresh start.

The Trinity

Christians believe in one God, but they also believe that God can be seen in three special, equally important ways. There is God the Father (the creator of all life), God the Son (who came to earth as Jesus Christ), and God the Holy Spirit (the unseen power of God, which is at work in the world). Together, these three are known as the Trinity. The Bible clearly tells of three "faces" of God, while stating that there is only one God.

Three fish as one Trinity

How Christians worship

Christians read the Bible and pray at home. Prayers are especially common before meals or at bedtime. Sunday (the day Jesus that rose from the dead) is the day that most Christians gather together in church buildings to worship. Church services include Bible readings, singing, and prayers. The church leader may give a sermon, a special talk about some aspect of Christian life.

An Orthodox bishop wears these clothes.

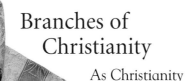

Branches of Christianity

As Christianity has grown, some groups of Christians have had different ideas about church practices and rules. Sometimes these groups formed new churches under the "umbrella" of Christianity. This is why we have many names for Christians, such as Catholic, Orthodox, Protestant, and Pentecostal. All have various customs and ways of worship, but share the same basic beliefs.

Following Christ

These Christians in Central America wave palm branches and follow a statue of Christ to celebrate Palm Sunday. In the short time that Jesus was teaching (about three years), he was followed by similar crowds, who heard his parables (stories with a message) and saw his miracles—amazing events that cannot be explained.

Caring for others

Jesus told people to love and care for each other. Christians may follow his teachings by performing acts of kindness, or by supporting or working for agencies that help people in need. This nun, who has chosen to devote her life to serving God, has opened an orphanage and hospital in Brazil to care for many homeless children.

Rites of passage

In most Christian churches, babies are welcomed into the church family at a baptism ceremony, when the baby is dipped in, or sprinkled with, water that has been blessed. Young Christians may also celebrate First Communion. This ceremony remembers a special meal that Jesus shared with his disciples the night before his crucifixion.

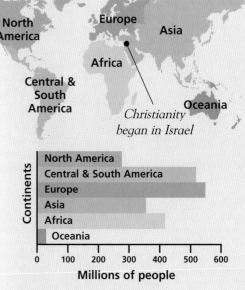

Main festivals

Epiphany The visit of The Three Wise Men to baby Jesus *January*
Ash Wednesday The beginning of Lent *February/March*
Holy Week: Palm Sunday, Good Friday, Easter Day Remembers Christ's life, death, and resurrection *March/April*
Pentecost Celebrates the coming of the Holy Spirit *June*
Advent Period leading up to Christmas *November/December*
Christmas Birth of Jesus *December*

Where Christians live

North America
Europe
Asia
Africa
Central & South America
Oceania

Christianity began in Israel

Continents: North America, Central & South America, Europe, Asia, Africa, Oceania
Millions of people: 0 100 200 300 400 500 600

Christians live throughout the world. Just under two billion people belong to one of the several dozen major branches of the Christian faith. The largest group is the Catholic church, which has about a billion members.

First Communion

REMEMBERING JESUS' LAST SUPPER

MY NAME IS ANTONINO and I am 10. Soccer is my favorite sport because it's a team game and many children can play together. The church I go to is a Catholic church in the square in our village. The thing that interests me about my faith is Jesus' commandment that we love and forgive each other. This year, I received the sacrament of First Communion.

Wine chalice

Bread

Antonino from Italy

The Last Supper

was the meal Jesus ate with his Apostles the night before he died. He gave them some bread and wine said that they were his body and his blood. I think it's important to take Communion because it is a way to meet Jesus.

My first confession

was a month before First Communion.

Everyone in my Catechism class went to church together. I sat opposite the priest and confessed my little sins to him. I was excited because it felt like I was face to face with Jesus.

I prepared for Holy Communion.

For three years I went to Catechism classes for one hour a week. They helped me learn more about Jesus. On the day of my First Communion, I wore a white habit, like all my friends. We were happy because we were about to take Holy Communion for the first time.

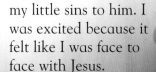

Before Mass, the priest called us into a side room.
We were all feeling nervous, but he reassured us. When we went back inside the church, the priest said a prayer for us. He wished us always to be good, pure, and ready to help our neighbors, as Jesus did. When it was my turn to receive the bread and drink the wine, I was nervous but happy at the same time.

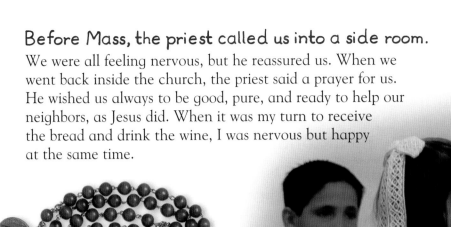

It felt like I was face to face with Jesus

A rosary is a treasured First Communion gift.

First Communion Bibles often have white covers.

After the ceremony I felt more grown up.
This was because my emotions were so strong. At the end of the service, everyone wished each other well. Then my family celebrated at a restaurant. My godfather gave me a computer as a gift.

When I'm older, I will be confirmed.
That is the way that a Christian can confirm his faith in Jesus. I am looking forward to my confirmation, since it will be me who decides when I'm ready to receive the Holy Spirit and show that I belong to God properly.

In some countries, Catholics take a saint's name, such as St. Francis, when they are confirmed.

Hector

Jola

Poland
I was a bit scared that something might go wrong at my First Communion, but it was fine. When I had the bread in my mouth I felt moved. I felt clean and new. I will never forget it.

Spain
At my First Communion, we all stood in front of the altar with pieces of paper that listed our sins. We burned the papers to burn our sins away and purify our souls.

Janine

Germany
For my First Communion I wore a long white dress. I was excited, but nervous. We had group lessons to prepare ourselves. We played, painted, sang songs, prayed, and talked together.

Christmas

CELEBRATING JESUS' BIRTH

Corinne from Sweden

I AM AN 11-YEAR-OLD called Corinne. Horse riding is one of my favourite hobbies. I love it! I also play the cello. My family goes to a kind of Baptist church. I think the praise songs are the best part of the service. My faith makes me feel loved and that I am never alone. Christmas is my favourite festival, but it's not because of the presents. It's because Jesus was born about 2,000 years ago. The best thing to happen to the world is our saviour, Jesus Christ.

Advent means "arrival". The four Sundays of advent lead up to Christmas. We put a star and candles in the window. We have four candles on our table and light a new candle every Sunday.

In Sweden we celebrate St Lucia's Day.

This special day is on December 13th. In my school, the older children visit us and sing songs. All the girls dress in white, wear wreaths, and carry candles. The girl who is Lucia stands in the middle. She has a crown of lighted candles on her head and a red belt around her waist.

We act out the Christmas story.

These nativity plays tell the story of Jesus' birth in a stable in Bethlehem. The church I attend has a Christmas play each year. The children act out all the parts. I was a dancing angel one year. The dancing made me so happy.

Lois

Germany

Advent is the preparation time for Christmas. On Christmas Eve, my family and I are very cheerful. We sing songs and go to the church service in the evening.

Jan

UK

Christmas for me is a time of celebration, but I also think about children throughout the world who are less fortunate than myself.

Music for a Christmas carol

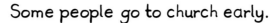

Some people go to church early.
They go to church for a Christmas service before the sun comes up. Everybody is happy because of the joyful news that Jesus was born on earth. People share their joy and sing special Christmas carols. Sometimes my relatives and I read the gospels on Christmas Day.

We have a special Christmas dinner.
I help with the cooking. There is lots of good food to share. I like the meatballs best. At four in the afternoon, we open our presents.

I bake gingerbread with my brother

Epiphany is 12 days after Christmas.
It is the day that the three wise men brought gifts to the baby Jesus by following the star. We celebrate this day with a service in our church.

The wise men followed a bright star to find Jesus and bring him their gifts.

Monica

Singapore
On Christmas Day our whole family spends time together. We go to church and watch the nativity play, which is extremely interesting. I enjoy the atmosphere as people sing hymns and greet each other happily.

Easter

HOLY WEEK

I AM EVA AND I'm 13 years old. I go to a Greek Orthodox church. I enjoy the moment when the old ladies gather round the priest at communion. My faith teaches me that there is one God, who cares about me. God cared so much that he sent his son Jesus to live on earth. At Easter, we remember how Jesus died, and after three days lived again.

Eva from Greece

Olives, feta cheese, and olive oil

The 40 days of Lent begin on Pure Monday.

This is when we remember the time Jesus spent alone and hungry in the desert, preparing to spread God's message. We have to make a sacrifice like Jesus did. My family and I do not eat dairy products or meat until Easter Sunday.

Small palm-leaf crosses

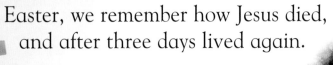

At midnight the priest announces the resurrection of Christ

After Mass on Palm Sunday we are given small branches of laurel.

My mother tells me that palm crosses used to be distributed instead. This is because Jesus rode into Jerusalem on the Sunday before Easter. People laid palm branches on the ground to honor him.

The Friday before Easter is Big Friday.

This is the day Jesus was crucified. During Mass, the priest takes the statue of Jesus' body from the cross. He puts it in a wooden box, which symbolizes the tomb. Women and children decorate the tomb with flowers. Later, the priests parade around the church with the tomb. We follow, holding candles and singing sad hymns.

On Saturday we gather for Midnight Mass.

We hold white candles, which are not lit. At twelve o'clock the priest announces the resurrection of Christ, and at that moment we light our candles. The children throw a lot of fireworks. Then we go home with our candles still lit.

My favourite Easter food is a kind of sweet bread called tsoureki.

It is made from flour, sugar, and milk. The Easter feast was held at my grandfather's house in the garden. We cooked a whole lamb on an open fire. The preparation had to start at 6 a.m.

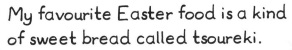

Plaited Greek Easter bread

Hard-boiled egg dyed red

Cracked eggs symbolize new life

We crack open the red eggs on Easter Sunday.

I crack my egg against someone else's. As I hold my egg I say, "Jesus is resurrected". The other person says, "He really is". In Greece, we colour the hard-boiled eggs during Holy Week. They are red because they symbolize the blood of Christ.

Greek Orthodox priests carry paintings of Christ.

Danilo

Serbia
On Palm Sunday we make wreaths with grass that has been laid down on the floor of the church. We do this while the service is going on.

Shirli

Albania
I like Easter very much. I also like red eggs. My grandmother has told me that eggs are symbols of life. I play the game of knocking red eggs with my cousins. During Easter, what I like most in church are the songs.

Priests lead a procession after Mass on Easter Monday.

They carry the church standards (flags), crosses, and candles, as well as icons (paintings) of Christ. They march in a procession that gets larger and longer as more people join in. The week after Easter is a very holy time. Monday is a national holiday in Greece.

Sunday service

A DAY OF PRAISE IN A PENTECOSTAL CHURCH

MY NAME IS HANNAH. I am eight years old, and I have a younger brother and sister. My faith makes me feel happy and excited. My favorite celebration is Christmas. My family share with each other by buying presents and having lots of fun and food. Every week we go to church to worship. The best part of the service is Sunday school. That's where I do my Bible studies. I also like the preaching because the pastor makes me laugh. We listen and try to do good so that our faith will help us every day.

Hannah from Ghana

Sunday feels special to me because I learn more about the Bible

We praise God with songs.

People play along on instruments such as the piano, guitar, drums, and bass. Our service begins with prayer and then we dance and sing and thank God for all he has done. Sometimes it gets very noisy.

Baptism opens the way to the Holy Spirit.
In the Pentecostal church, people are baptized in water. This is an outward sign that everyone can see, but it is what is happening inside the person that is important. When the Spirit enters our bodies, we may be able to heal others, speak in tongues, or tell about the future.

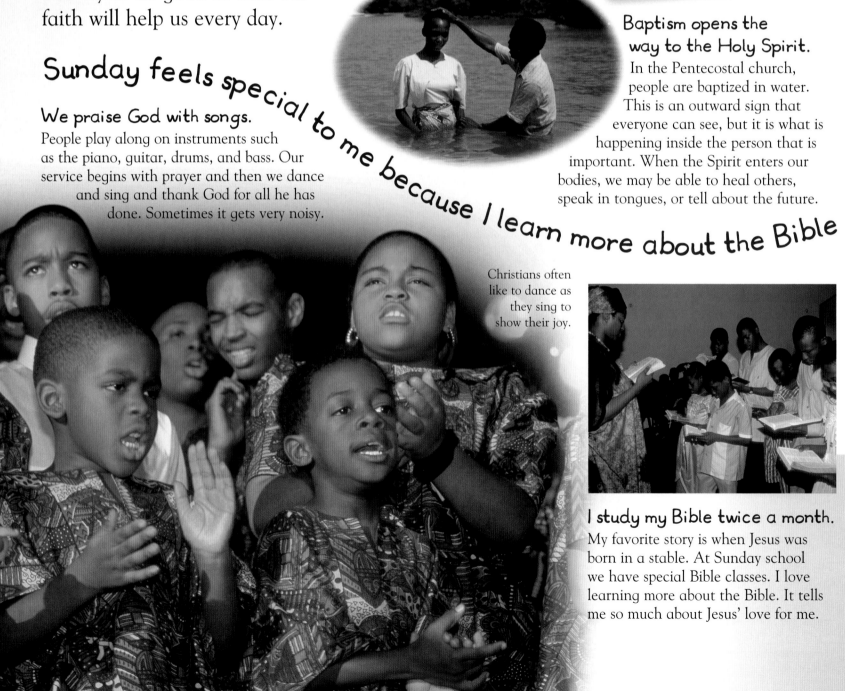

Christians often like to dance as they sing to show their joy.

I study my Bible twice a month.

My favorite story is when Jesus was born in a stable. At Sunday school we have special Bible classes. I love learning more about the Bible. It tells me so much about Jesus' love for me.

My mom and dad speak in tongues when they pray.

Sometimes the Holy Spirit fills people with such joy that they talk in a different language. This is called speaking in tongues. The first time I heard it, I thought, What is this? It doesn't sound like a language.

Jesus' disciples received the Holy Spirit first and then prayed in tongues.

Some churches are big and have a separate entrance for Sunday school.

People wear nice clothes for church.

Some people wear clothes that look expensive. The pastor sometimes wears a suit. Our service is about one-and-a half hours long. After prayers and music, we listen to sermons about God. Then we praise and worship God with more music. After church, I play with my friends and my brother and sister. Sometimes we go out to eat.

Prayer makes me feel blessed.

Sometimes a person who is praying for you will lay their hands on your head as they pray. This is called the laying on of hands. When I have been prayed for in this way, it makes me feel very happy.

Jamaica

I like singing and dancing, Sunday school, and learning about God. I like to be with the people at Sunday school. I like songs about God because I love him.

Shanté

Symbol

The crescent moon and star symbol has come to represent the Islamic faith. Some mosques, and many flags of mainly Islamic nations, feature this symbol. It has no religious meaning, but it may have been chosen because the Islamic calendar is based on the phases of the moon. In the Islamic calendar, each year has 12 months of 29 or 30 days for a total of 354 days. A new moon marks the start of each month.

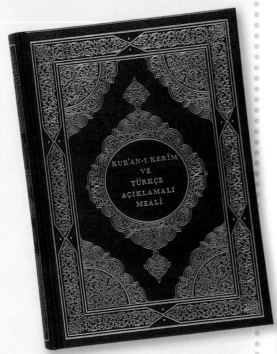

Holy book

Muhammad memorized God's words and taught them to his companions, who wrote them down in a book called the Qur'an. This book contains descriptions of God and his powers, as well as rules about how Muslims should live. Many Muslims try to learn Arabic so they can read and recite the Qur'an in its original language.

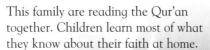

The arrow on this special compass (called a qibla) points towards Mecca. Muslims must face Mecca to pray.

Islam

FIVE TIMES A DAY, all over the world, followers of the Islamic faith stop what they are doing and pray. With each prayer, they show their devotion to God, most often called by his Arabic name, Allah. Today, there are more than a billion followers of Islam across the world. The word Islam means "surrender to God", and followers of this faith (known as Muslims) must obey God's will. The religion's holy book, the Qur'an, contains the word of Allah, as told by an angel to Islam's founder, the prophet Muhammad.

This family are reading the Qur'an together. Children learn most of what they know about their faith at home.

How Muslims worship

Muslims worship God by reciting the Qur'an and praying five times a day at certain hours. They recite prayers in Arabic, although they can also speak to God in their own languages. People worship at home, or pray with other Muslims in a mosque. Before they enter the mosque, all Muslims must remove their shoes and wash their faces, arms, and feet. On Friday, the Islamic holy day, everyone gathers in the mosque to pray.

Islam's founder

Muslims believe that Muhammad was chosen to hear God's words and teach them to others. Born in Mecca (in present-day Saudi Arabia) in 570 CE, Muhammad taught that there is only one God, who created and controls everything in the world.

The written word

The Qur'an is the word of God, so it must be written with great care. Many Muslims practise a beautiful style of handwriting, called calligraphy, so that their writing can be as special as the words themselves. Calligraphers use brushes and coloured inks to create this decorative writing.

Places of pilgrimage

Mecca, Muhammad's birthplace, is the holiest place on earth for the majority of Muslims, called Sunnis. They travel to Mecca on Hajj (a pilgrimage) at least once in their lifetime. The other main branch of Islam (about ten per cent of Muslims) is called Shia. Many Shi'ites regard the city of Karbala, in Iraq, as their primary place of pilgrimage.

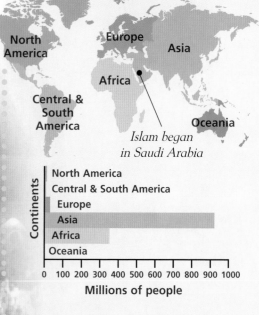

Thousands of Shi'ite pilgrims journey to visit the Imam Hussein mosque in their holy city of Karbala.

The Five Pillars of Islam

Muslims have five sacred duties to perform as part of their faith. They must recite words of faith, pray five times a day, give help to the poor, fast during the month of Ramadan, and travel to Mecca at least once in their lifetime. These duties are called the Five Pillars of Islam.

Muslims kneel on a special mat to pray.

Rites of passage

The first sound newborn Muslim babies hear is their father whispering the call to prayer (called the *adhan*) in their right ear. When the baby is seven days old, parents have a naming ceremony, the *aqiqah*. They may shave the baby's hair, and make a special offering to the needy. As they grow older, children are taught about Islam at home and at the mosque.

Main festivals

Day of Hijra New Year *(1st month of the Islamic calendar)*
Mawlid al-Nabi Muhammad's birthday *(3rd month)*
Laylat al-Qadr Night of Power *(9th month, towards the end of Ramadan)*
Eid al-Fitr Celebrates the end of Ramadan *(10th month)*
Dhu al-Hijja Hajj *(12th month)*
Eid al-Adha Festival of Sacrifice *(12th month)*

Where Muslims live

Islam began in Saudi Arabia

Nearly a third of all Muslims live in North Africa and the Middle East, but the majority of Muslims live in central and southern Asia. Smaller populations live in the West.

The Five Pillars of Islam

THE FIVE DUTIES OF A MUSLIM

I affirm my faith daily.

Every time I hear the call to prayer from the muezzin, I say the words, "There is no god but Allah, and Muhammad is his messenger." This first pillar shows my faith in Allah.

I AM RACHID, and I am nine years old. I like playing soccer and listening to music, and some day I want to visit the city of Marrakech. Islam is the religion I know about. It teaches me how to be good with people and behave in a nice way. It only takes me five minutes to walk to the mosque nearby. I often go there during the week and always go on Friday because it is a holy day. The Five Pillars are important because they are the things all Muslims must do to show faith and respect to Allah.

Rachid from Morocco

1. For me, facing Mecca is where the sun rises. We begin with the words, "Allah Akbar" (Allah is greater than all else).

2. We bow our heads to show respect for Allah. Another verse is spoken from the Qur'an. In the mosque, the imam says the words. If I'm praying at home, I say them.

3. Next, we place our foreheads on the prayer mat in a very deep bow, called prostration. This shows that Muslims are humble in Allah's presence.

4. Then we kneel on our prayer mats to pray silently to Allah. This finishes with a prayer for the community.

5. Finally, we turn our heads left and then right, wishing the peace of Allah to all people.

I concentrate more when I pray at the mosque.

The second pillar says you must pray five times a day. The call to prayer always comes from the mosque. There are big speakers on top of the minaret so that everyone can hear the muezzin's call. Before we pray at home or in the mosque, we perform wudu. This means we must wash our faces, arms, and feet. Then we face Mecca to pray. I have my own sheepskin prayer mat at home.

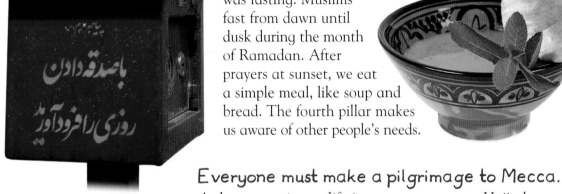

We must help the poor and needy.

The mosque is a community and there are always some people who need extra help. Paying *zakat* means giving money to help others. It is the third pillar of Islam. If you don't have a lot of money, you don't pay a big zakat, but everyone has to give something. Visiting sick or needy people is another way to do this duty.

Turkey
In Istanbul where I live, children do not usually go to the mosque. They receive their religious guidance from parents or grandparents. As we get older, we start to pray more and become closer to God.

Cemi

Money to help the poor may be put in a box at the mosque.

The Five Pillars show respect for Allah and other people

We fast as Muhammad did.

When the angel brought the word of Allah to Muhammad he was fasting. Muslims fast from dawn until dusk during the month of Ramadan. After prayers at sunset, we eat a simple meal, like soup and bread. The fourth pillar makes us aware of other people's needs.

Khulud

Everyone must make a pilgrimage to Mecca.

At least once in our lifetimes, we must go on Hajj, the pilgrimage. This is the fifth pillar. People travel to Mecca and put on simple clothes so that everyone is equal. They go to the Sacred Mosque and circle the Ka'ba shrine seven times. Then there is a festival to celebrate the end of Hajj.

Germany
On Friday I always pray at the mosque. There are many people and the men pray separately from the women. The call to prayer must be really loud so that everybody can hear it.

The Ka'ba is a cube-shaped building covered in a black cloth.

Ramadan and Eid al-Fitr

A MONTH OF FASTING FOLLOWED BY A FEAST

Water

Fresh dates

MY NAME IS LEENA and I am nine years old. I have two sisters who are older than me. I like drawing and playing basketball, and I want to be a vet when I grow up because I like animals. This year, Ramadan was very special for me. For the first time, I fasted for the whole month with my family. Then Eid al-Fitr arrived and we all celebrated. It is one of the most special days of the year.

Leena from Jordan

During Ramadan we still go to school.

Muslims must not eat or drink from dawn to dusk. This is called fasting, and it is one of the greatest acts of worship to Allah. It was a bit difficult to study at school for exams during fast days, but the teachers were understanding and didn't give us extra homework. The main thing we did at school was collect money to buy clothes or food for poor families.

We eat before dawn.

The day's fast begins once we hear the call to dawn prayer. Apart from the last couple of days, I didn't feel tired or hungry. We break the fast at sunset by eating dates and drinking water.

The holiest night of Ramadan is Laylat al-Qadr, the Night of Power. This is the night that Allah sent the Qur'an to Muhammad. Muslims stay up all night to worship in mosques or at home. I stayed up until 2 a.m. praying. Allah said this night is better than a thousand months.

Giving money to the poor is important.
During Ramadan and Eid, we try to help a little more. Our mothers cook food and we help to share it with children in the orphanage. We also collect and distribute blankets, heaters, and clothes, and donate money at the mosque.

Mosque alms box

A new moon is the start of a new month.
We wait for a new moon to show us that Ramadan has ended and the Festival of Eid can begin.

We remember Allah and feel his nearness more than any other time

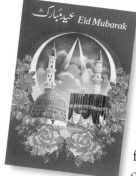

We send Eid cards to family and friends.
We send them cards because they live abroad and are too far away to visit us for Eid. On the night of Eid we always phone our family and friends to congratulate them.

We welcome people to our home during Eid.
My sisters and I wear new clothes to welcome our visitors. We offer them Arabic coffee, sweets, and chocolates.

We have an Eid lunch with our closest family.
For lunch, my mother makes stuffed chicken, and Arabic rice mixed with minced meat, carrots and peas. It has fried almonds, raisins, and pine nuts on top. During the meal I get scared a few times, thinking that I should be fasting. Then I remember that now I can eat during the day again.

Afghanistan
Ramadan is a special time for Muslims. Muslims fast for one month to remember that everyone is equal. Poor people don't have food, so everyone fasts to know how it feels if you don't have food.

Omar

UK
Eid is a celebration of the end of Ramadan. To celebrate, we visit our families and we go to fun fairs. I also like visiting aquariums.

Yasmin

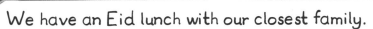

Living by the Qur'an

ALLAH'S RULES FOR EVERYDAY LIFE

I AM INÈS. I don't have any brothers or sisters, but I have a best friend and about 30 cousins. I love going on holiday with my family. Sometimes we visit relatives in Algeria and Morocco, but I've also been to Kenya, Mexico, and New York. There is a mosque near where I live. Inside there is lots of beautiful Arabic writing from the Qur'an on the walls. We have several Qur'ans at home. The holy book contains Allah's wishes for how we live our lives. All Muslims should live by these rules.

Inès from France

The Qur'an is Allah's word.
We treat the Qur'an with respect. The copy at my mosque is kept on a stand. We read the words on the page from right to left. Allah's words are special, no matter how they are written.

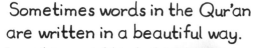

Writing a copy of the Qur'an is an act of devotion.

Sometimes words in the Qur'an are written in a beautiful way.
I see this special kind of Arabic writing on prayer mats, on buildings. and in some copies of the Qur'an. It's called calligraphy. No matter where Muslims live in the world, they read the Qur'an in Arabic.

Soshi

Bangladesh
At Eid al-Fitr we have to wake up early and pray. The food is great (curry and chicken tikka). I like this Muslim festival because it is a joyful time.

Afghanistan
The Qur'an tells all the rules on how to live, like don't have a boyfriend or a girlfriend, and do what your mum and dad tell you. It's important to eat halal food. Maybe I'll learn to speak and write Arabic when I'm older.

Andaleep

I show respect for older people.

The Qur'an teaches me to do this. I am lucky because all my grandparents are alive. We go to visit them five or six times a year. I think you should respect older people because they have lived a long time and learned a lot. I like hearing them talk about what they were like when they were young.

Muslims dress modestly when they go out.

The Qur'an tells us that we should dress in a certain way. Some Muslims are stricter than others, but most girls I know usually wear a scarf over their heads. From the age of 12 they must cover up most of their bodies, apart from their face and hands. Boys might wear a cap on their heads.

These girls are all wearing head scarves.

Legs and arms should also be covered.

Someday I want to try to learn the words of the Qur'an by heart

I'm learning to read Arabic.

Some children go to a Qur'anic school (madrasah) inside a mosque, but I go to my local school. I go to school every Saturday for three hours to memorize the Qur'an. My friends say it takes a long time. Muhammad memorized the words of Allah when the angel Gabriel spoke them to him. So doing this yourself is a way to honour Allah.

We only eat certain foods.

All the foods we can and cannot eat are described in the Qur'an. Muslims are not allowed to eat pork, drink alcohol, or taste blood. Muslim butchers kill animals in a way that helps drain the blood away. When we want to buy meat we go to a halal butcher.

Hajj and Eid al-Adha

A SPECIAL JOURNEY TO THE HOLY CITY OF ISLAM

Mohammed from Dubai

MY NAME IS MOHAMMED, and I'm 13 years old. My faith makes me feel peaceful and secure. I go to the mosque every day. Friday prayers are especially important, and all men must pray in the mosque. My father, brother, and I never miss this. My favourite place in the mosque is standing in the first three rows behind the imam because these are the people that Allah will be looking at. One of the things that Muslims must do is to worship Allah by going on Hajj, a pilgrimage to Mecca. Hajj is one of the Five Pillars. Eid al-Adha is the feast to mark the end of this special journey.

Hajj is when Muslim pilgrims set out to visit the Ka'ba.
The Ka'ba is the holy house of Allah in the Great Mosque. It is covered in a silky black cloth, and decorated in gold with verses from the Qur'an. In the corner of the Ka'ba is a stone that has fallen down from heaven.

Hajj is a religious duty.
Muslims who can afford to make the journey, and who are healthy, must go at least once in their lifetime. Young children don't usually go on Hajj, so they can learn about the importance of the pilgrimage by performing a mock Hajj in their local mosque.

A black cloth covers a reconstruction of the Ka'ba shrine.

Children dress as pilgrims and circle the shrine seven times.

Pilgrims wear white robes called Ihram.

Tents are set up for the pilgrims.

Muslims camp near holy sites.

Hajj takes place over several days so that pilgrims can visit all the sites. They must walk seven times between two small hills near the Ka'ba. On the second day of Hajj, they visit a place called Arafat. The pilgrims must pray there until sunset and be alone with Allah. They must also throw pebbles at stone pillars (representing Satan).

Pilgrims have certain rituals.

To get ready, they put on simple white robes, wash, and declare their devotion to Allah. They pray as they walk seven times around the Ka'ba. A final ritual is for women to trim their hair. Men cut theirs shorter or shave their heads. My father and uncle came home with shaved heads.

Everyone drinks the sacred water.

Every pilgrim goes to the ancient Zamzam well to drink the water. Before they drink, they make a wish. With Allah's will, it will come true.

Bottled Zamzam water

Hajj demonstrates our belief in one God

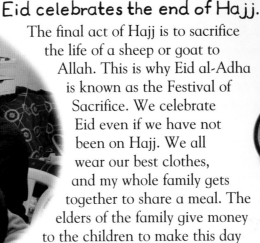

Eid celebrates the end of Hajj.

The final act of Hajj is to sacrifice the life of a sheep or goat to Allah. This is why Eid al-Adha is known as the Festival of Sacrifice. We celebrate Eid even if we have not been on Hajj. We all wear our best clothes, and my whole family gets together to share a meal. The elders of the family give money to the children to make this day even more special. It makes me happy.

Ma'moul biscuits

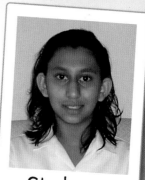

Dried yogurt balls

Shabnam

Turkey

Hajj is visiting the Ka'ba. Ka'ba is the house of Allah in the holy city of Mecca, and visiting this special place strengthens unity, equality and brotherhood. I hope to go there when I am a bit older.

Emre

Junaid

India

In Islam, you have to go on Hajj at least once in a lifetime. I would love to go to Mecca because you will be able to eat anything. It would be very fascinating to see the Ka'ba and to see a great big mosque.

South Africa

I love Eid because my whole family is together. We share gifts and sweetmeats. I also love it when we change into our new clothes.

OTHER FAITHS

ALONG WITH THOSE WHO practice the major
world religions, there are smaller numbers of
people across the globe who believe in other
faiths. Some of these religions are based on
ancient traditions. Others have been
introduced fairly recently. These pages will
introduce you to some of these faiths.

These Korean women dance
in traditional costumes during
Sokchonje, a spring festival
for followers of Confucianism.

Zoroastrianism

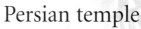

PERHAPS THE OLDEST faith still practiced, Zoroastrianism is also one of the least well known. About 150,000 people (mostly in India) are followers. Zoroastrians believe in a supreme God named Ahura Mazda, the creator and the source of all that's good in the universe. They believe that people can overcome evil in the world be doing good deeds, thinking good thoughts, and living a good life.

Symbol

The Farohar symbol has three layers of feathers to represent the three pillars of the faith: good works, good thoughts, and good deeds. The circle at the center signifies the founder of the faith, Zoroaster.

Persian temple

These boys chat outside an ancient temple in Persia (modern-day Iran) that is decorated with carvings of Persian soldiers. The Zoroastrian place of worship is called a fire temple. Inside, priests keep a sacred fire burning constantly. Some of these fires are are said to be centuries old.

The sacred shirt

Boys and girls whose parents are Zoroastrians join the faith in a special ceremony. The child wears a sudreh (sacred shirt), a plain white garment that symbolizes purity and good will. The kushti (sacred thread) is wrapped three times around the child's waist. Both items will protect the child as he or she tries to be good.

Altar of fire

Zoroastrians worship in front of fire because Ahura Mazda is the source of all light in the world. At home, they keep a pot of fire burning because rituals and prayers (said five times a day) must take place in front of it.

Shinto

THE ANCIENT RELIGION of Japan is known as Shinto. It is practiced only in Japan. Many Japanese Buddhists also follow Shinto rituals. The faith has no founder, but is based on traditional practices. Shinto means "the way of the gods". Its followers believe that there are millions of gods (known as kami) all around, which have supernatural powers. People worship the kami at shrines.

Hundreds of wishes

People usually visit a shrine—either a home, a local, or a national shrine—to mark special events or celebrate holidays. They write prayers on cards and tie them to a tree at the shrine for the kami to grant their wishes.

This Shinto good-luck kami, called Daikoku, is worshipped by Buddhists as well.

Symbol

This beautiful gate is a torii, a symbol of Shinto. The torii invites people to enter a shrine and worship. The gate may also stand alone as a shrine in itself in a place of natural beauty.

Drumming to the kami

This Shinto priest bangs a large taiko drum, known for its thunderous roar, in Kyoto, Japan. When people enter a Shinto shrine, they may clap their hands together to get the kamis' attention. Priests bang their drums outside the shrine to tell the kami that there are worshippers present.

Obon festival

Shinto believers respect their elders. At Obon, or the Festival of the Dead, the souls of their ancestors are said to return home for a visit. People visit graves and leave offerings. At the end of Obon, huge bonfires are lit to bid the souls goodbye for another year.

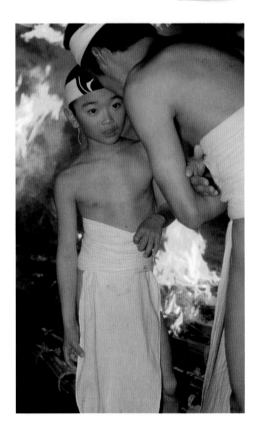

Taoism

TAOISM IS A FAITH that helps people to understand the energy, or power, that connects all living things. Tao means "path", or "way", like "way of the world". A Chinese philosopher, Lao-tzu started Taoism in the 6th century BCE. Taoism is a personal faith, and it is up to each person to come to understand Tao.

Taos try to lead good lives and not harm others. Some Taos believe in gods and goddesses, who bring them good fortune and watch over what they do.

Symbol

Taoism is represented by the yin-yang symbol. It shows two opposite forces at work in all things. For example, yin is darkness and yang is light. The dots of one color inside the other show that a small part of each force exists within its opposite.

The three ways

For more than 2,000 years, the three main religions of Buddhism, Confucianism, and Taoism have coexisted in China. The faiths have taken ideas from each other, as well as from the ancient religious rituals of China.

The founders of three religions: Buddha (left), Confucius (center), and Lao-tzu (right)

Tai chi

This man is doing a set of movements to help the power of Tao flow through his body. Tai chi looks like an exercise, but to Taos it is much more than that. Tai is the power in everything, and chi is the flow of energy. When people do Tai chi they bring together all their inner strength and energy.

Taoist believer performs Tai chi outside a Taoist temple in China

Ways of worship

Personal worship, such as meditating and chanting, or praying in front of an altar at home, are important in Taoism. There are also religious services led by priests at temples. A temple may be dedicated to one or more gods. There is usually an altar inside, which worshippers face as they pray.

Symbol

Jains do not worship a god. Instead, they follow the examples of the 24 Jain teachers, known as Tirhankaras. Statues like this of the teachers are found at temples and shrines.

Jainism

MEMBERS OF the faith known as Jainism believe that everything they say, do, and think has an effect on their lives. They also respect life and must not harm any living things. Jainism is an ancient religion that began in India. Today, most of its five million followers still live there.

Jain art

This is a statue of Mahavira, the sixth-century Indian who started Jainism. Jains believe that he was the last of the great teachers who lived in the distant past. Here, his statue is being washed (see below).

Respect for animals

Ahimsa (noninjury) is important to Jains. They are strict vegetarians and try never to kill animals. Jain monks even cover their mouths to avoid breathing in tiny insects.

Jainism shares many ideas with Hinduism, including a respect for animals.

Statue-washing festival

Pilgrimage to a holy site is important in Jainism. Every 12 years, Jain pilgrims gather at a temple in southern India for a statue-washing festival. Paraders wear elaborate and colorful costumes, and priests pour pots of coconut water and fragrant spice pastes over the statue.

Jain parade held once every 12 years near Jaisalmer, India.

Baha'i

THE BAHA'I FAITH BEGAN about 150 years ago in Persia (modern-day Iran). Its followers believe that there is one God for all people. He might be known by different names to people of different faiths, but Baha'is feel that everyone worships the same God. They also believe that all people are equal and that they belong to one human family. So the goals of the Baha'i believers are to spread the ideas of unity and world peace.

Symbol
The three interlocked triangles in this Baha'i symbol represents how all people and all religions are united. The symbol is also a nine-pointed star. Nine is the number that stands for unity.

House of worship

Baha'i has no religious leaders. Instead, respected members of the church conduct the service. They usually gather in believers' homes to worship and pray, but Baha'is may also make a visit to a house of worship. Most have nine sides, and many are topped with guilded domes.

Baha'i gardens

Houses of worship are usually surrounded by beautiful gardens, as the founder of the faith, Baha'u'llah, wished. This garden is part of the Shrine of the Bab in Haifa, Israel. Baha'u'llah, along with his teacher, Bab, founded the faith in 1863. He gathered his followers in a garden near Baghdad and announced that he was a prophet sent to guide them.

Lotus Temple, Delhi, India

Glossary

Alms A gift of money or other offerings to help the poor, or to pay for the work of the church, or to support monks and nuns.

Ancestor A member of your family who lived a long time ago, before your grandparents

Angel In many religious traditions, an angel is a spiritual being who helps and serves God or the gods. An angel is often a messenger.

Artha This Hindu term means trying for success, usually at school or at work. Artha is one of the four goals of life.

Baptist A member of one branch of the Christian faith, the Baptist church. Baptist believers are baptized as adults, they follow the word of the Bible, and share the duty of church leadership among the congregation.

Bar Mitzvah A Jewish celebration for a boy when he is 13 and joins the congregation. Bar Mitzvah means, "Son of the Commandments". When Jewish girls are 12, they join the church by celebrating their Bat Mitzvah "Daughter of the Commandments".

Bimah A raised platform in a Jewish synagogue from where the service is led, and the Torah is read.

Bishop In Christian churches, a person who is given the job of overseeing priests or ministers in matters both spiritual and practical.

Catechism In the Christian faith, a handbook of questions and answers that sum up the faith's beliefs and practices. Children learn about their faith by memorizing the questions and answers in catechism classes.

Catholic This word means universal, but usually describes a member of the Roman Catholic church, a Christian faith that celebrates Mass, and accepts the voice of a leader called the Pope as the word of God.

Ceremony An activity that is performed on a special occasion, often in a very formal and elaborate way.

Challah bread A braided egg bread, served at the Jewish Sabbath meal and at holidays.

Community A group of people who share the same faith, for example.

Confirmation In the Christian church, a ceremony performed by a bishop to renew or confirm a person's faith in God. It is usually done from the age of 12, or in early adulthood.

Crucifixion An old method of execution, in which the victim's hands and feet are bound or nailed to a wooden cross. The Bible tells us that Jesus died this way.

Custom A specific practice that has long been accepted.

Devotion A feeling of strong commitment to something; a willingness to serve God.

Dhamma In Buddhism, the name for all the teachings of the Buddha, which form the ultimate truth.

Dharma This Hindu term means doing your duty. Dharma is one of the four goals of life.

Disciple Followers or students who believe in, and help to spread the ideas of, their leader. In Christianity, for example, Jesus had 12 disciples.

Divine Something that is devoted to, or comes from, God.

Enlightenment An awakening into a much greater understanding of faith and the world around us. In Buddhism, a person who reaches this goal is truly free and can live a deeply religious and thoughtful life.

Fast To go without food, or avoid certain foods, for religious reasons.

Faith Another word for religion, faith also means complete trust and belief in an idea or person.

Festival A special day or days in the religious year that are set aside for celebration and feasting.

Gatka A martial art practised by Sikhs. Gatka is also the name for a stick used to practise sword fighting.

Gospels In Christianity, the four books in the New Testament of the Bible (Matthew, Mark, Luke and John) that tell the story of Jesus' life.

Guru A religious teacher or guide.

Holy Something that belongs to or is set apart for God or the gods. People, objects, festivals, and places may all be described in this way.

Hymn A song that is specially written as a song of praise or prayer, typically sung to God.

Kama In the Hindu faith, finding enjoyment, often seen as music, dance, art. Kama is one of the four goals of life.

Karma In the Hundu faith, where this term originated, the idea that all the good and evil that a person does will return, in this life or in a later one. Many Buddhists also believe that a person's actions determine their future destiny.

Laws A set of rules people should follow as they deal with each other. The Jewish Torah, for example, sets down laws for Jewish people.

Mahayana The traditions of Buddhism practised in China, Japan, Korea, and Vietnam. Mahayana teaches people that they must find the path to enlightenment themselves, but that it is just as important to lead others to enlightenment.

Mass The celebration of the Eucharist (or Holy Communion), usually used in the Roman Catholic church.

Meditation A state of relaxing and concentrating, so that the mind can focus on spiritual thought.

Mela An Indian religious fair or festival.

Minaret A tall, slender tower built next to or in an Islamic mosque, from which the Muslim people are called to prayers.

Moksha This Hindu term means the release from the cycle of life and death. Moksha is the fourth goal of life.

Monastery The community and home of monks or nuns living together and practising their faith.

Muezzin In Islam, the person who calls Muslims to pray five times a day.

Novice A person who has entered a religious order (for example, monks or nuns) but has not taken final vows.

Offering Money, food, flowers, or some other gift given to the church or other place of worship to show respect and give thanks.

Orthodox (Christian and Jewish) This term is used to describe a traditional faith, in which there are set ways to observe the faith that are not changed.

Parade A long procession that includes people marching.

Passover The Jewish festival celebrating the flight of early Jewish people from slavery in Egypt.

Pentecostal A member of a faith within the Christian church that puts special emphasis on the gifts of the Holy Spirit, such as the ability to heal or speak in a holy language.

Prayer A way of communicating with God. Some prayers have set words that are used every time and not changed.

Preach To deliver a sermon, a special talk usually based on sacred texts to help encourage and instruct the faithful.

Priest A spiritual leader, who often has the authority to carry out religious rites or ceremonies.

Prophet Someone who can interpret the will of God.

Prostration A very deep bow, performed by touching the knees, hands, and forehead to the ground to show extreme respect.

Protestant A group of faiths within the Christian church. Historically, Protestants in northern Europe tried to reform the Catholic church in the 16th century, and eventually broke away from it altogether.

Rabbi A spiritual leader in the Jewish faith, the rabbi is a scholar and teacher who is an expert in understanding Jewish law.

Reform In the Jewish faith, this term describes Jews who adapted their faith to live in the modern world.

Reincarnation The belief that a person's soul does not die, but is reborn over and over again as a different human, an animal, a plant, or an object.

Relic A special object (such as a bone or tooth) that is connected with a religious figure, and is treated with great respect.

Respect To think highly of and show honor toward.

Resurrection In Christianity, the rising of Jesus on the third day after he was crucified on the cross.

Ritual Any of the customs or practices in a religion or religious ceremony.

Rosary In the Catholic faith, a string of prayer beads containing five sets of ten small beads, each separated by another bead, and a crucifix. People use the beads to count prayers as they say them.

Sabbath A day of rest and worship. For most Christians, this is a Sunday; for Jewish people Saturday; and for Muslim Friday.

Sacrament A religious act giving the grace of God to those who receive it.

Sacred Anything that is believed to have a special purpose or connection to a faith.

Sacrifice The practice of offering food, or the lives of animals or people, to God, as an act of worship.

Scripture The written texts that are believed to be sacred in any religion.

Service The music, prayers, and rituals when people gather in a house of worship.

Seva In Sikhism, the goal of serving and helping others, especially the poor.

Shiite The second-largest tradition within Islam. Shiites reject the caliphs (chief Muslim leaders), and believe that Muhammad's cousin Ali (and his descendants) followed Muhammad as leaders.

Shrine A place of worship that is closely linked with a sacred thing or person.

Soul The part of a person that is not their body, but may be thought of as the very thing that makes a person who they are.

Spirit A supernatural being or force that many people believe exists all around us.

St Lucia A young Christian martyr (someone who suffers or dies in the name of religion) who is recognized as a saint in the Catholic and Orthodox Christian church. In Sweden and Norway, her life is celebrated in a midwinter festival of lights.

Stupa A Buddhist temple. When this form of architecture spread to China, it was changed slightly to form the pagoda.

Sunni The name for the largest tradition within Islam. When Muhammad died, there was a divide among Muslims about who should lead them. The Sunnis believe that the caliphs were their rightful leaders. They believe that they are the true followers of the prophet Muhammad. See also Shiite.

Symbol A real and visible object that is used to represent something that may be invisible (for example, an idea).

Temple The home of a god; a place of worship.

Theravada The only one of the early schools of Buddhism that has survived to the present day, especially in Sri Lanka, Thailand, and Burma. Theravada focuses on personal responsibility.

Tradition A custom or practice passed down from generation to generation.

Vegetarian A diet that includes food that comes from plant sources, but limits or eliminates food from animal sources.

Vow A serious promise, sometimes between God and a person.

Worship A feeling of profound love, honor, and devotion. Praying, attending religious services, reading sacred books, or making offerings are all ways of worship.

Wudu In Islam, washing with clean water to prepare for the daily prayers.

Index

Credits

The publisher would like to thank the following for their kind permission to reproduce their photographs:

Key: a=above; b=below; c=center; l=left; r=right; t=top;

akg-images: 42bl, 57cl, 62tr; Gerard Degeorge 68br; Suzanne Held 74l; Erich Lessing 61tl; Jean-Louis Nou 25bc; Alamy: allOver Photography/TPH 57br; Paul Doyle 35cr, 36ct; Fotofusion Picture Library/Christa Stadtler 69br; Sally & Richard Greenhill 4tr, 62cr, 67cr; Image Solutions 30b; Israelimages/Israel Talby 4tl, 43tr, 50tl, 51c; Norma Joseph 25bl; Lucky Look/Thore Johansson 56tr; Steve Outram 58tr, 59tl; Gabe Palmer III 8r; ReligiousStockOne 59r; Anders Ryman 4tc, 55tr; Janine Wiedel Photo Library 69tl; World Religions Photo Library/Osborne 41bl, 60c, 67tr; www.jpsviewfinder.com/photo by Jean-Philippe Soule 74br; ArkReligion.com: Jon Arnold 43bl; Dinodia Photo Library 12cl, 76r, 77b; Itzhak Genut 45cr; Chris Rennie 65tl; Helene Rogers 3tr, 14tr, 15tl, 17cl, 32tl, 32bl, 32br, 34br, 36bl, 45c, 45bl, 47cr, 48br, 55cr, 58cr, 71tr; Trip 65b, 71tc; Bob Turner 17tl; Bridgeman Art Library: Cameraphoto Arte, Venezia 42c; British

Library: Add. 5589 f.111 6tl; Corbis: Paul Almasy 7bl; Nathan Benn 72; ChromoSohm Inc/Joseph Sohm 60bl; Dennis Degnan 50br; Owen Franken 7br, 51tl; Free Agents Limited 29b; Michael Freeman 12cc, 25br; Gallo Images/Luc Hosten 48cr; Farrell Grehan 1; Lindsay Hebberd 14cr, 18c, 19tr, cr, 31tr, c, 53tl, 73bl, 76c; Robert Holmes 20bc;Angelo Hornak 76tl; Jeremy Horner 18l, cr; Earl Kowall 73bc; Earl & Nazima Kowall 9tr; Charles & Josette Lenars 8bl; Chris Lisle 24cl, 28cl, 76bl; Craig Lovell 19br; Stephanie Maze 53b; John & Lisa Merrill 6bl; Milepost 9 _/Colin Garratt 62tl; Richard T. Nowitz 45br, 47br, 48bl; Christine Osborne 8tl, 63tr; Caroline Penn 23tr; Mark Peterson 49c; David Pollack 10bl; David Reed 49tr; David Samuel Robbins 22tl; Royalty-Free 12bl; Anders Ryman 24bl; Ariel Skelley 56c, 57cr; Roman Soumar 34tl; Ted Spiegel 56bl; Penny Tweedie 8c; David H. Wells 48tl; Corbis/Reuters: 52br; Gopal Chitrakar 3tl, 12tr; Amit Dave 15b; Zainal Abd Halim 71tl; Dipak Kumar 37tl; Savita Kirloskar 73cr; Yoriko Nakao 27tr; Ajay Verma 41br; Corbis/Sygma: Jacques Langevin 33tr; Desai Noshir 6tr, 35t, 39c, 40b; Patrick Robert 61cr; DK Images: British Library 68c; British Museum 22cl; Burrell Collection, Glasgow Museums 52tr; Judith Miller / Ancient Art 46cr; St Mungo, Glasgow Museums 12cr, 12br, 38bl, 63c; The Museum of London 63tl; Empics/EPA: 26tl, 35cl; Eye Ubiquitous/Hutchison Library: 64tl; Nigel Howard 28tl; Liba Taylor 51tr; Gamma/Katz: Remi Benali 31br; Gantier Marc 74tr; Wallet Patrick 20r; Job Roger 53br; Koren Ziv 77cr;

Getty Images: Lonely Planet Images/Juliet Coombe 42tl; Photographer's Choice/Angelo Cavelli 26c; Uriel Sinai 44br; Chung Sung-Jun 27c; Taxi/Gavin Hellier 13b; The Image Bank/Yann Layma 75bl; Ami Vitale 71cl; Getty Images/AFP: 14cl; Anatolian News Agency 7tr; Jimin Lai 69tr; Karim Sahib 62br; Gent Shkullaku 58b; Getty Images/Stone: Andrea Boher 21tr; Bushnell/Soifer 46tl; Rex Butcher 75r; Sylvain Grandadam 74cl; Robert Harding Picture Library: Gavin Hellier 3tc, 23tc; Magnum: Bruno Barbey 30c, br, 54c; Panos Pictures: Jean-Leo Dugast 25t; Mark Henley 70b; Ami Vitali 17cr; Powerstock: age fotostock 17tc; Reuters: Munish Byala 37c; Kamal Kishore 41tl; Gil Cohen Magen 44tr; Manish Sharma 36br; Yun Suk-bong 27l; Rex Features: 66b; Stefano Caroffi 34bl; Sipa Press 70tr; The Travel Library 30cl; Peter Sanders Photography Ltd: 64b; Still Pictures: Hartmut Schwarzbach 29b; David Towersey: 52cl, 55cl, 58cl; World Religions Photo Library: 13tr, 16tr, 33tl, 36bc, 38br, 39tl, tr, 40cr, 54cl, 60br, 73tl; Gapper 26bl, 51br, 61cl.

All other images © Dorling Kindersley
For further information see: www.dkimages.com

Dorling Kindersley would also like to thank:
John and Anne Angood, Xenophon Ankrah (60tr), Michelle Gordon, Harrington Hill Primary School, Matilda Marks Kennedy School, Selwyn Primary School, Roma Sheen, Rajesh Shrestha (24tr)